Heart Sense

Heart
Sense

Unlocking Your Highest Purpose
and Deepest Desires

Paula M. Reeves, Ph.D.

Foreword by Robert Romanyshyn,
author of *The Soul in Grief*

CONARI PRESS

First published in 2003 by Conari Press,
an imprint of Red Wheel/Weiser, LLC
York Beach, ME
With offices at:
368 Congress Street
Boston, MA 02210
www.redwheelweiser.com

The author gratefully acknowledges permission to excerpt from the following:
From *The Essential Rumi* by Coleman Barks with John Moyne. Copyright ©1995 by
Coleman Barks, used by permission of HarperSanFrancisco. Excerpt from "Sudden
Chartes," *The Book of Roads* by Phil Cousineau. Copyright © 2001 by Phil Cousineau,
used by permission of Sisyphus Press.

Library of Congress Cataloging-in-Publication Data

Reeves, Paula M.
    Heart sense : unlocking your highest purpose and deepest desires /
Paual Reeves.
        p. cm.
Includes bibliographical references.
    ISBN 1-57324-819-3
    1. Spiritual life. 2. Women—Religious life. 3. Heart—Religious
aspects. 4. Self-realization—Religious aspects. I. Title.
    BL625.7 .R44 2003
    291.4'4—dc21
                                    2002151860

Cover Collage and Book Design: Suzanne Albertson
Typeset in Bembo.
Printed in Canada
TCP

10 09 08 07 06 05 04 03
 8 7 6 5 4 3 2 1

To my sister, Evelyn, whom I've
carried in my heart since childhood,

And to the newest heart link in our
family, our grandson, Ryan

HEART SENSE

FOREWORD

"Do you have the heart for living your life as fully as you are able?" This a question that Paula Reeves raises in the third chapter. It is also a fair statement of the challenge that this book places before you. You cannot read this book in a neutral way. As you are reading it, you will find that it is reading you and that in subtle yet powerful ways, it is calling you to live your life more fully, authentically, and creatively. In this respect, *Heart Sense* is a work of art. Like all art, it tempts you beyond the fixed boundaries of your everyday ways of living. So beware! Do not read this book if you do not wish to be disturbed from the comfort of a life lived in distraction. On the other hand, do read it if you already know somewhere deep within your heart, the longing that knows without knowing that you are in exile away from yourself and searching for home.

Twenty years ago, I began a journey toward the heart with a book that described that moment in time when the heart became a pump. It has been a long road on which I have tried to be a witness for the losses we have suffered on a collective, cultural level by reducing the heart to this image. But it was not until I experienced the anguish of grief over the unexpected death of a spouse that I was drawn more deeply into the heart of the matter. In the winter of mourning, I heard my heart speak the language of tears, and I heard in those liquid words how grief endured can open the heart to deep pools of compassion and can be the seed of a transformed capacity for love. When the heart breaks open in sorrow—a theme that Paula explores so beautifully in chapter eight—the deep and dark roots of love are exposed. In this moment of exposure, one comes to realize, as the poet Rilke says, that love is the most difficult work of all. And yet, as the psychologist Veronica Goodchild notes, love is also the one experience that we would not want to miss before exiting this life. When the heart breaks open, love becomes more than valentine sentiment. In the wounded and broken heart, love blossoms as the capacity to hear the appeals of the other, including the other that we are within our own hearts. Within the heart of grief, love becomes the start of a journey of homecoming—heart work as homework.

Heart Sense is a love story. It is a compassionate and humane invitation to know yourself, and a wise and gentle appeal to lose your mind for the sake of finding your heart. Should I strike this last sentence? Should I avoid those words and phrases that might seem too provocative and too extreme? No, I think not. We are in exile, individually and collectively, and we are living in an age of terror, poised at the edge of an abyss from which we are called back most often by grief. Witness the worldwide outpouring of grief when Princess Diana died, or the collective sense of sorrow that continues today around the events of 9/11. I wonder if grief is the last refuge of the dying heart and its ways of knowing and being, the last experience that might awaken us before we tumble into the abyss. Have we become so insensitive to the heart's voice that now only the shock of terrible loss will awaken us from the sleep of reason—a sleep in which we have forgotten that the heart has its reasons that reason does not know? Alongside mind and its capacities to know the world from a distance, have we forgotten that the reasons of the heart are the seasons of the soul, which web us into the fabric of all creation?

One of the real values of *Heart Sense* is that it answers this question about grief with a resounding "No!" We do not have to wait for traumatic moments of loss and grief to find the heart, either individually or collectively. This book restores the broken connection of mind and heart and offers multiple ways in which each of us can begin to hear the whispers of the heart. The chapters invite you to meet your heart, come to know what it knows and wants, to know what it loves and lives and celebrates. Paula offers multiple ways in which each of us can tap into the rhythmic, seasonal wisdom of the heart and find there the courage—a word that is rooted in the etymology of the word "heart"—to live life as fully as possible, with grace, compassion, and joy. For me this gift has been humbling and transformative.

I call this book a love story because it marries mind and heart, intelligence and compassion, content and style, theory and practice. Paula's "Heart Notes" offer exercises involving matters of the heart that root you in the heart of the matter. She is a sure guide who meets you more than halfway in your places of exile. Her words touch you simply but honestly, like the reassuring gesture of a friend's hand on your shoulder. Reading her book, you are walking with such a friend, one who also has a good ear and who knows how to listen with heart. Along this path, I found myself slowing down, and I would advise you to savor slowly the wisdom of her words. Open your heart to what is here. Resist the temptation to race ahead and get the information. Let the book get you. Let yourself slip into reverie as you read because then you will discover, as Gaston Bachelard, the great teacher of reverie notes, you have entered into the soul's dreaming rhythms.

There are many oases in *Heart Sense*, places along the way where you stop and are nourished by what you have heard. Of all these many places, there was one that moved me to tears. In the third chapter, Paula describes how the mitochondrial DNA connects all women to the mother line. She explains that every women can know that "her body carries a record of maternal blood bonds within every cell linking her without refute to first woman, first mother, first daughter, first birth, first body record of incarnation." And then she adds that although experienced differently, every man can participate in this wisdom of the heart and feel the presence of the family of humankind. Through the tears of grief, I once knew that connection of heart to the larger story. This book helped me to remember that feeling. Thank you, Paula.

—ROBERT D. ROMANYSHYN, PH.D.

ACKNOWLEDGMENTS

The seeds for this manuscript began to sprout when I first read the contributions to the field of energy cardiology made by Drs. Linda Russek, Gary Schwartz, and Paul Pearsall. My fond appreciation to them for watering the soil. Later, the many contributors who freely shared their personal experiences kept embodied my faith in what I was writing about. These are ordinary folks living the results of these stories in creative and life-sustaining ways. Their generosities allowed this manuscript to blossom. To the many retreat participants with whom I have had the privilege of working, you truly produced the fruits of this labor. Nationally and internationally, you have taught me that the heart knows no boundaries of race, ethnicity, or gender. Bless you.

My gratitude to my editor, Leslie Berriman, who herself is a woman of great heart, unerring sincerity, and a fine sense of humor. Her willingness to take every exercise to heart kept my pen and my focus on track. To Conari Press, my publisher, who continually reminds the world that random acts of kindness unite and heal us, I offer thanks for keeping me closely attuned to the basics of love and relationship.

To Pam Suwinsky, the book's copyeditor, whose discernment has distilled and refined my prose, my continued appreciation and delight in her finishing touch.

To Annette Cullipher, whose vision gave birth to Journey into Wholeness, which has allowed so many of us to explore, in community, the deep yearning of our hearts.

To my husband of fifty years, Don Reeves, who gave me many hours of his computer expertise without complaint or reminders that the hour was late. His encouragement has been my mainstay.

To my family, whose five generations have shown us all what in life counts and what is truly superfluous, I owe my sense of faith that life is worth living and that when the time comes, handing the task over to those who follow is both a blessing and a privilege.

And to the readers of my first book, whose enthusiasm and feedback have inspired me to keep writing—thank you.

CHAPTER 1

How to Use This Book

Tell me, can you love life and let love find you
when you are lost?
—ORIAH MOUNTAIN DREAMER

O f all the organs that make up the human body, the heart and the heart alone is considered to be the guardian of the complex emotion we call love. Love, our heartfelt attraction to another and our heartfelt acceptance of ourself, has deep and tangled roots. It begins in utero with a unique blood bond when this life-giving fluid is exchanged between the heart of the fetus and the heart of the mother. From conception on, this bond is complex. The mother's blood is the foundation for the uterine lining to which the fetus must anchor itself. The health of the mother's lifeblood determines the health of that first fetal environment. Even as the fetus's liver begins to manufacture its own blood supply, the mother's steady heartbeat orients this new life to the rush and roar of the maternal heart's functions. This bond not only keeps the fetus alive, but it allows the fetal heart to record the biochemical messages that will prepare it for other kinds of bonds—emotional, physical, spiiritaul, and psychological—after birth. The prenate's heart is being prepared for a capacity for love, compassion, and empathy. After birth this original heart-to-heart relationship has to widen and develop sensitivity to others if the infant is to relate to the rich and varied complexity we perceive as life.

As children, we are taught logic and reason as the primary tools for discerning the accuracy of our perceptions. But few of us are encouraged to listen to our hearts, whose nonverbal responses may at first be less clear but are far more unbiased than those of our brains. There is no surer way to find out whom you are truly meant to become—your life's purpose—than by learning to listen to your heart. Across the years, as your life grows increasingly more complex, your heart can guide you as you seek to identify your true self. To ignore your heart-centered input would be a major loss.

Over and over our heart gives us nudges and clues about our unlived or ignored life possibilities. What we learn too late in life is that the very qualities and talents that we so want to support or that we admire in others are the very talents and qualities that we know in our heart are right for us. Any time I find myself admiring a particular quality in another person, I always turn to the intelligence of my heart and ask myself, "Where is this quality or talent hidden away and yet to be claimed in me?" And equally, any time I find myself strongly disliking someone or something about another I turn to my heart and ask, "Where is this attitude or trait or *fear* in me?" I have never found this question not to yield a meaningful, and often life-changing, response. The way of heart-centered living is unabashedly honest—it is not for the timid or the indifferent pilgrim.

Reducing Heart Stress by
Reclaiming the Wisdom That Is Yours

We live in a very stressful world. The everyday necessities of living, like commuting, jobs, and children, require more flexibility and attention to intrapersonal resources like fortitude, faith, courage, and confidence than ever before in our history, as we are drawn ever deeper into a global community. Daily we are faced with decisions and choices unique to these times—many of which we feel ill equipped to manage. Most of us intensify our search for answers when we are under stress—feeling caught up in the complications and pressures that surround us. During this period of time the rhythms of our brain and our heart become out of synch with one another; we feel this as a lack of focus, an imbalance of mind and body.

Your body radiates energy called an electromagnetic field. You know when it is working well and in balance because you feel centered and filled with energy. Your heart's electromagnetic energy is 5,000 times stronger than that of your brain. In fact, research shows that your heart has its own capacity for intelligence that is controlled neither by the brain nor by the autonomic nervous system. No one can yet explain exactly why the heart is able to beat independently of control by the brain or the influence of the nervous system, but it does. Energy cardiologists tell us that the heart has its own "little brain" that enables it to act independently of the big brain and to produce feelings, directions, and solutions all on its own.

As you learn to access and trust the wisdom of your heart's intuitive intelligence, you will find that your brain and heart rhythms will become smoother, more synchronized, just as they do with a feeling of deep love, or meditation, or beauty. Even if you are in distress, accessing this capacity for heart guidance will immediately begin to reduce your stress level, especially if you are able to combine it with the genuine intimacy of relating to another, heart to heart. When you feel related, you also feel renewed, reassured that you are more in tune with the depths of your own humanity. No matter how frightened or ill you may be, you will feel empowered by the inner sense of unity that your sharing brings.

A clear example on a national scale of this immediate heartfelt healing response under dire circumstances was our instinctual reaching out on September 11, 2001—to strangers, to friends, to family—to anyone who was willing to meet us heart to heart. Our intellects could not grasp the enormity of our loss. Our hearts could.

Simply turning and listening to the heart that loves you is one of the most protective things you can do for yourself and for humankind. The entire world seeks healing—healing begins with love and love begins with bone-honest relating—from the heart.

So let's look at how you can use this book to get to know yourself intimately from the depths of your heart while uncovering your destiny, your unlived life.

The Purpose of This Book

First, I have written this book to help you uncover the unlived truths in your life, to find what your heart can tell you about your soul's purpose, about your destiny, that you are unaware of or yearning for but afraid to create. Layer by layer you will carefully brush away the debris of your mistaken beliefs and unearth your deepest self by turning to your heart and its intuitive intelligence.

This book is simply written, but its message is anything but simple. It is serious, it is sincere, and it is absolutely real. Whether you believe it or not, your life has a purpose that transcends your ordinary everyday existence. *You have a soul that is alive and vitally present within every cell of your body and that can be found very readily by turning to your heart.* This incarnate energy is intelligently and eternally connected to Universal Soul, whether you call this Spirit, Brigid, God, Sophia, Buddha, or pure chance. Your dreams, your yearnings, even your addictions and your symptoms are all ways in which your soul is speaking to you about your essence—your core self. I am inviting you to develop a relationship of love with That Which Loves you through your heart's wisdom and unplumbed energy. I am inviting you to recognize how deeply you are loved so you can look at stranger and friend alike and find a soul connection.

I believe every life has an unlived purpose. It's called *destiny*. If you are fortunate enough to recognize this purpose and live it consciously, intentionally, your life unfolds in a deeply fulfilling manner. Joseph Campbell, author and mythographer, in referring to a person's revitalizing connection to this inner source of direction coined the phrase "following your bliss." Living even a portion of your life's purpose is the closest you ever come to true happiness—to bliss. Your dreams, your yearnings, even your symptoms can give you insight that will help you identify your unlived desires—your destiny. Does this guarantee you'll never have a heart attack? Of course not. What it does do is strengthen your personal sense of purpose which increases your sense of well-being which improves your immune system which reduces your stress which is not a bad way to live at all.

Second, and maybe of even greater importance, I have written this book out of an ongoing concern about the rapid increase in heart disease in our culture. Heart attacks and strokes, once believed to be largely a male health problem, have become a significant factor in the quality of everyone's health, especially during our later years. Many factors contribute to this growing concern about the increase in heart disease. For example, as life expectancy increases, it is important that we cultivate ways to reduce overtaxing the heart in order to enhance the quality of life in elderhood. Knowing ourselves well at an early age from the depths of our heart surely will help. In this book I explore how the unlived life of our dreams and our yearning contributes to the stress that damages our heart's healthy functioning.

Another example is the number of heart attacks that occur shortly after the workday has begun on Monday mornings. Social scientists have strongly suggested that when a person feels trapped in a deadening and demoralizing job that she must keep in order to survive, the psychological and physical results negatively affect her heart. In other words, the heart simply breaks.

Heart disease isn't limited to physiological influences alone. What we think, what we feel, whether we perceive ourselves in this world as effective and autonomous beings or ineffective and choiceless victims plays a very large and influential role in our heart health. In our technologically advanced society, with its emphasis on cure, the very real statistic that heart disease is the number one killer of women is often obscured by the continuing debate about hormone replacement therapy (HRT) and its contribution to heart health versus its effect on cancer and osteoporosis. This debate in and of itself continues to create enough stress among women trying to determine whether to undergo HRT that it has probably contributed more to poor health than to providing clear information that would reduce stress and allow for a confident and informed choice.

You will find some of the simplest and most healing principles for claiming and maintaining your heart health in the pages that follow. Even if you have had a heart attack or have heart disease, these principles will decrease your stress and allow you to live a deeper and more fulfilling life. Too many of us repress our grief until we have a broken heart and then, frightened, do all we can to further disguise the body wisdom that is teaching us openly and consciously to claim our grief in order to strengthen, not weaken, the heart. Too many of us defer our heart's desire for a later time—some day—somehow—and meanwhile we live lives of quiet desperation or sadness as we watch the magical *someday* pass us by. Meanwhile we learn to ignore the heartache and live with the stress it engenders.

The Organization of This Book

This book is written so that you can take your time with a single chapter, or a single topic, and then spend a week (or more if you care to) working with the exercises called Heart Notes that appear throughout each chapter. These exercises will help you discover how to recognize your Heart Sense and discover your unlived life. This format is intentionally designed to inspire a deeply personal exploration of your life's purpose from which you can glean deep insight, draw strength, and take delight. You will want to provide yourself with a journal just for recording your work with the book's exercises.

Each chapter contains contributions from readers who have begun this exploration themselves. The entire book is written in an easily read conversational manner, with stories that offer something for everyone.

The chapters are divided into different categories of heart sensing, like What Your Heart Loves, When Your Heart Is Broken Open, and so on. Chapters 2 and 3 (The Seventh Sense and Meeting Your Heart) are especially important because they provide an overview about our cultural and scientific symbolism and misunderstandings concerning the heart and soul. They present two foundations that firmly ground this book. The first is that while we moderns are inclined to regard the soul and destiny as mystical or unfounded in truth, these concepts have deep and enduring historical roots. The second is that your physical body is a small personal model of the cosmic universe. Your cellular body reflects a multitude of the "mystical" truths of the ages. Both of these foundations lead to one truth—that your soul is an *embodied* reality whose presence and purpose is expressed by your heart's energy. Further, in these two chapters I discuss how science is showing us evidence of this truth.

After reading these two chapters I am confident you will agree that it is self-diminishing for anyone today to neglect to know and celebrate the extraordinary intelligent spiritual complexity that is the body. It is a significant personal loss to scoff at intuitions or be self-deprecating about one's embodied wisdom. One might call me an "embodied feminist" I feel so adamant about resacrilizing the body and its wisdom.

In the following chapters, I will explain how to access your embodied language and insights from a number of perspectives, each designed to allow you to resacnlize your relationship with your essential self.

Chapter 2: The Seventh Sense asks you thought-provoking and soul-searching questions about your personal relationship to your heart in order to help you begin to discern the presence of heart-centered messages.

Chapter 3: Meeting Your Heart lays out the relationship between your physical heart and the emotional bonds that are created by its energy. This chapter explores the importance of the in utero blood bond between the fetus and its mother and how this bond develops into a cellular capacity for trust and openness. Also, we explore how doubts and fears block your ability to access your intuition.

Chapter 4: What Your Heart Knows discusses the relationships among dreams, emotions, and the ability to calm yourself. Identifying what your heart *knows* will enable you to discriminate between a broader sense of wisdom about your entire life and the more selective guidance of what your heart *wants* concerning selective choices from the general range of insights and possibilities.

Chapter 5: What Your Heart Wants introduces you to Sharon and Marianne and their questions about the difference between fate and destiny. This chapter teaches you how to value, honor, and make manifest those signals that are life changing. You will discover that many of the places and activities that you find attractive are actually reflective of your soul's preferences.

Chapter 6: What Your Heart Loves invites you to differentiate between *who* you love and *what* you love. This chapter looks at the complexity of love and its many meanings as they affect your life.

Chapter 7: Where Your Heart Lives invites you to soul search and describe the geography that your soul vibrationally responds to. You will be asked to imagine how you might literally live in one of the geographical places you love and, if you cannot, to imagine how you can create some of that environment where you live now. We will discuss travel as sacred and place as reflective of your inner terrain.

Chapter 8: When Your Heart Is Broken Open takes you into the realm of deep grief and inexplicable loss. You will learn how to allow your heart consciously to break by uncovering the depth of your capacity for feelings, and how to do this with meaning in order for you to expand your relationships and take in life fully. We talk about grief and healing and resiliency and deep sorrowing.

Chapter 9: When Your Heart Celebrates reminds us of the wide variety of experiences that the heart's knowing celebrates throughout the entire life cycle, from birth to death and beyond. This chapter will remind you of all that you have uncovered during your ever-deepening relationship with your heart-centered wisdom, emphasizing the strength and self-awareness that comes with consciously creating the rituals that celebrate life and death.

Working in a Recovery or a Self-Exploration Group

If you care to use this book in a six- or eight-week, two hours weekly, workshop or group format for members of a heart health or self-discovery group, the participants would read the chapter at home on their own and then come to the group either to do the exercises or discuss their experiences having done the exercises at home.

Because this book is both a guide toward a deeper relationship with your heart and contains a great deal of new information about your soulful embodiment, it can also be used as a text in a discussion format. Reading one chapter at a time and then discussing it in a group can take from eight to twelve weeks.

When I teach this material I use a heart-centered body prayer, Spontaneous Contemplative Movement, with movement, music, and art. You may wish to incorporate similar activities into your group's work. A list of possible music choices is included in the Resources at the back of this book.

CHAPTER 2

The Seventh Sense

. . . Before the art of medicine comes the art of belief;
but before either comes the art of being.
—DEEPAK CHOPRA

Heartwarming, heartache, heartless, heartbroken, heartfelt: our language is laced with the pulse and expressive beat of the heart's metaphoric presence. Rarely do we complete an entire day without encountering some symbolic reference to the heart. And there is never a week that passes without numbers of men and women either dying of heart-related disorders or being diagnosed with heart-related disease. Advertisers rely upon the heart's universal message as an undeniable life force to soften our resistances, luring lovers to turn to its evocative throbbing appeal, while writers, poets, and musicians rely upon the heart's pulsing cadences to lend vitality to lyrics, poetry, and prose.

Beginning with an oral tradition and continuing with the written word, humankind has persisted in an attempt to make meaning from experience and then tell the story from a personal perspective. From Richard the Lionhearted to Oz's Tin Man—who was convinced he only needed a heart to feel complete—the bits and pieces of story, ballad, myth, and metaphor remind us that the human heart is central in describing a meaningful experience. Most often recognized because of its muscular, organic, life-giving blood surges, your heart is also a central force behind a vitality that is less pragmatic, more poetic, more mystical and soul gifting. Life viewed through the heart's lens reflects connection to a greater cause, a broader relational view of life. Further, reflecting upon life from the heart's perspective *can save your life!* Your heart literally is responsive to all you think and feel. It is central to the depth and the shallowness of your emotions. Further, it is as responsive to the inactivity of your spiritual life as it is to the activity of your brain. Every mood swing, every jarring thought, every loss, pain, or joy engages your heart and influences its efforts in your behalf. The quality of our daily life fluctuates according to our heart's intelligence and energy. *We live or die according to our relationship with our heart.*

Every moment of our waking life and during most of our sleep we are guided by the information we gather through one or more of our senses. Our senses are so vitally important to our feelings of wholeness that when one fails us the others become keener and more adept at gathering the information that would have been available through the absent sense. The five most familiar senses—taste, touch, smell, sight, and hearing—are joined by a sixth—intuition—and influence every decision and every choice we make. In our sleep we turn to the cellular remembrances gathered via our senses, which are then recreated in our dreams as images. If asked, we would probably say we think our way through life, but in truth, we *sense* our way.

Philosophers, spiritualists, the religious, and others have spent their lives exploring and seeking the source of soul, of embodied transpersonal wisdom that has inclined every culture to name and venerate a godhead onto whom the projections of the mysterious presence of this wisdom can be fastened. Across the centuries every exploration has returned again and again to the metaphors of the heart, as if poet and cleric alike surmised that the human heart was more than a cellular organ. Casually we exclaim, "Bless my heart!" when we are surprised or feeling vulnerable. We use the irrefutable integrity of the heart when we give an oath "upon my heart" and are quick to emphasize the impact of a situation by expressing that "my heart is broken." As we learn more and more about the intelligence of our hearts we are beginning to realize that these expressions are grounded in our embodied sense of the heart's responses and reactions. These responses and reactions are such a major contributor to our sense of physical and emotional well-being that when we turn toward this intelligent inner source we find a *seventh* sense—heart intelligence. This seventh sense speaks to us physically and spiritually. In fact it may be the ultimate integrative vitality that helps us live our lives as spiritual beings. The contemporary evidence of the effect the heart plays in life validates the beliefs of those who have preceded us. Ancient myths, rituals, and admonishments that to the Western scientific community seemed to be artifacts of superstitious practices, poetic fancies, or pagan mysticism now are being viewed in a different light. This seventh sense, especially, may be council for the soul.

The Sixth and Seventh Senses

The traditional division between body and mind no longer makes sense. The old map that limits the human experience to only five senses is clearly no longer adequate. Quantum physicists have shown us that we are more, much more. We are, they say, an interactive intuitive energy system with many unexplored areas of communication, of relating, of knowing. Our experiences far exceed the capacity of the five senses alone, even when they are combined with the rationality and logic of the thinking mind. Dreams, emotions, imagination, intuition, and images are very real ways of making meaning as we cross the threshold into the splendors and the chaos of the twenty-first century. Feelings are real; dreams carry very specific guidelines for the dreamer, and in some cultures for an entire community. Intelligence is no longer locked up in our "gray matter." Intelligence is everywhere present and speaking to and through us via our multiple senses (taste, touch, smell, hearing, sight, intuition), our cellular responses, our heart's intelligent wisdom.

Humankind has relied always upon the information and guidance acquired by the five senses. Indigenous people further accepted what for modern humankind remains an ill-defined and often elusive sense, often called the sixth sense. The sixth, that inexplicable surge of suddenly knowing what moments before you had no inkling that you knew, is called intuition. It announces its presence complete and with no introduction. Our language recognizes this remarkable stepchild of the sensate family with expressions like, "I just had a hunch." Scientifically, intuition has been a thorny blossom in our sensory bouquet because it cannot be measured, as can the other five senses. Nor can it be located physically, as can each of the others. Where is intuition? In the gut feeling that warns you away from danger, the weak knee that underscores your vulnerability so it can't be ignored except at your own risk, or the absolute illogic of thinking of someone you have not heard from in ages and within a short period of time hearing from them?

In my first book, *Women's Intuition: Unlocking the Wisdom of the Body,* I take us to the source by teaching us to listen to the body and trust the metaphoric language of our symptoms, our spontaneous movements, our dreams. While sight, sound, taste, touch, and smell are faculties the body develops *to interact with the world,* the sixth sense, intuition, *is developed to interact with the universe.* And now there is yet another "sense." The *seventh* sense: The remarkable *intelligent* wisdom of your heart, which when developed allows you a more direct interaction *with your primary essential self,* your incarnate (embodied) soul.

For years I had lectured on the relationship between destiny and fate, telling my listeners that within each of us there is the knowledge of what we are truly capable of if we follow our soul's design. That deep within each of us there is a cellular knowledge—a nonverbal intelligence that is our gift in utero and that when brought to consciousness will lead us toward the fulfillment of our life's purpose. How to listen? How to hear that purpose is the more difficult part, so I'd coach participants in discovering their "Heart's Yearning."

Invariably we would begin our weekend gatherings in curiosity and by the end of three or four days, lives would have been changed, healing would occur, and the sense of community had grown richly. Then I began hearing what happened after the workshops ended: how lifelong attitudes were altered, relationships shifted, and even how more than a few people changed their lives completely as they were guided by what their heart was teaching them about their destiny, their life's purpose. On the other hand, if we choose to live our lifes without ever questioning what our essential nature—our deeper wisdom—is telling us, we will find ourselves living out not our destiny but our fate. We may live well but unconsciously, and when it comes time to die we will discover there was a vast *unlived life* that was begging to be fulfilled. I am not talking about material accomplishments, wealth, or acquisitions, although these may occur. What I am speaking of is the willingness to be sourced from within rather than led from without. A willingness to seek the capacity to turn inward and rediscover who you truly are and what your life is truly about.

Your soul converses with you in very practical ways. The consistent nagging feeling that you can't bear to have such a cluttered living space or ignore any longer the urge to get your finances in order is a soul message. Once you take your*self* seriously and make the change, you will be quite amazed at who you become unfettered by the nagging concern. A joyful centered life is all about sincerity and discipline—not rigidity—but focused change. This is one of those simple basic tenets of spiritual truth that appears too ordinary to give a second thought. Wrong.

The Heart Across Cultures

Some of history's heart-centered rituals appear more barbaric than others, yet we must acknowledge that the heart's potent influence has remained central, keeping alive our attention to its underlying meaning and leading us to where we are today. The Meso-American ritual (practiced primarily by the Aztecs from 1200 to 1500) of removing the still-beating heart from a live victim appears horrendous from a twenty-first-century perspective, yet the ritual reflects the cultural mythology that, in its own way, contributes to the history and meaning that were passed on to succeeding cultures. Barbaric or holy, each ritual continues across the centuries to remind us that a human life is more than just a tissue-and-bone existence. Since time began, there has been a reverence for the unknowable yet palpably present *something* that draws humankind into a search for soul. Each ritual became, for its culture, an enduring reminder that a human soul carries the seed of Eternity within it, and if that seed can be accessed through ritual or other means the culture will be better for it.

In the example used, many warrior cultures favored the hearts of their victims, removing them while still pulsing to use in some ceremonial manner. It was believed that as long as the heart remained beating, the potent energy and wisdom of the heart's vitality—represented in some cultures (Egypt and the Orient, for instance) as a dancing god—was available to the priest or priestess to use as he or she wished. We may shudder as we read about this ritual, but today we can transplant a human donor heart into a recipient and know with absolute assurance that the vitality of that organ is available to the new host. The dancing god dances now within a new breast.

Honoring the potency of this *mysterium* and its vital beat was so central in Eastern belief systems that Tantric sages imagined the heart as an incarnated container for the mysteries of the universe. There within its hallowed chambers the god Shiva dances, keeping alive the eternal rhythms of the Infinite. As the heart beat so beat the pulse of the Eternal. The heart was, they believed, vital to maintain the human link to the Eternal. A soulful umbilical to Universal Soul if you will.

The Symbolic Heart

On a lighter note, a friend recently disclosed to me that she was always fascinated by the small medallions of the Sacred Heart carried by her Catholic schoolmates. She began secretly collecting them. A shy child, she felt empowered by carrying one on her person. She said she began to touch this bit of silver whenever she felt sad or lonely or discouraged, confiding her feelings to it and listening for reassurance. Over time she was taught by her respect for the "energetic presence" of the sacred symbol that she must also become aware of her pleasures and especially her gratitude. Shyly and with a beaming smile, she said that she learned through this practice that most of her sadness was her own limiting perspective about what she imagined others felt or believed. "When I began to look into each situation for any small thing that I could have *genuine* gratitude for I began to feel more loving—and more loved!" And tapping her chest she said, "Today I carry that heart right here within my own heart. Its energy has danced me through my laughter, my sorrows, and my hard times. Sometimes the dance has been as slow and as heavy as a funeral dirge and sometimes I have felt like doing a jig."

What my friend didn't realize was that her ritual goes back to an ancient belief in the healing strength in the dance of the heart's beat.

Reared in a Christian church, she had no way of knowing that the early church had outlawed ecclesiastical dancing as a sinful practice to be avoided at all costs. In order to create a unique and separate identity, the church fathers had to sever any historical or ritual relationship with the revered dancing gods of "pagan" Egypt, India, or the Orient. It wasn't until the seventeenth century that an article of faith formally adopted the concept of the Sacred Heart, as if this recent approval completely severed it from its ancient mystical roots. This declaration supposedly ignored evidence that the heart as a sacred object in the Christian faith had continued alive and well in amulets, stained glass windows, and texts for several centuries prior to the church's ceremonial acceptance of its meaningful symbology. Cultures across the globe have kept some form of this belief alive in spite of the regulations of religion or science. Expunged, forbidden, or forgotten, all deep truths eventually reemerge in another guise to "speak" to the heart that has the wisdom to listen.

Additional Attributes

Still, there is more to the heart's attributes. For centuries civilizations have attributed the qualities of *judgment* and *justice* to the "heart" in an attempt to find meaning in suffering and error. Even in the highly sophisticated Egyptian culture we find the belief that at death every heart-soul has to descend to the Hall of Judgment and be weighed upon the scales of *Ma'at,* the keeper of cosmic and social order. The counterbalance of the sins accumulated by the *Ab* (the Egyptian word for the heart-soul, considered the most important of the seven souls bestowed upon an individual by the seven birth goddesses) during a person's lifetime must be balanced against a weight of truth. Supposedly the heart grows heavy with a lifetime accumulation of "sins." This final "weight" is measured against the featherweight of the soul. This process is often depicted as a scale with a tiny figure, or a heart, on one side and a feather on the other.

The Heart's Enduring Message

We may turn the truths of the past into sentimental stories or caricatures of paper and lace, but the messages bleed through. In Argentina the beautiful pink rosacrucia stone is harvested from the earth and often carved into the shape of a heart, given as a gift of remembrance, of friendship. In Mexico there are silver heart-shaped *milagros* (miracles) pinned to the Virgin's garments in supplication for a healing, a mending, a renewal.

In Egypt, the story of the god Osiris includes yet another version of the carved heart as reminder, a *talisman* to bridge the gap between what was and is now. Osiris was required to suffer a phase of death before he could be resurrected by the Goddess.

In the myth Osiris is torn apart metaphorically and put back together bit by bit to await the next stage of his journey. During this time he is referred to as "still heart." We are told that his mummified body received a red stone heart, which supposedly assured the human seeker of the promise of the eventual return of life's vitality after a life-changing challenge, albeit in a different form. We are *never* exactly the same after consciously facing a heartfelt change. Yet in spite of how our ego feels buffeted, our body depleted, our mind stretched, our heart and soul remain stalwart and ever with us no matter what. Whether you are ten or ninety when you look into your mirror, the eyes looking back at you will always contain the original spark of your soul, still burning steadily.

Not unlike what every human experiences with maturation, if Osiris was to evolve he could not escape the pain of psychological and spiritual dismemberment, of having to reevaluate behaviors, give up rigid and unproductive attitudes, and consciously accept the resulting changes. For the myth to have meaning, the human listener has to be able to identify with the story at a personally soulful level. In order to make meaning out of experience, to get to the heart of the matter, the sincere seeker is taught not to expect to find a panacea or an amulet that will guarantee a safe journey or protection from the pain and disappointments of life. That journey would be an unrealistic and unconscious one. It is pure fantasy to believe that if you do your inner work no pain or harm will befall you. What the sincere seeker can hope to find are the connections and the coincidences that tell her she is on a path with heart. And a heart-centered life will prepare you for whatever life requires of you, now or later.

In Hawaii, I'm told, there is a ritual of praying *from* the heart. Wordlessly the group focuses on the breath and the heart's energy and waits for their hearts to pray—to express what the mind cannot. There is a universality to prayer from the heart. A profoundly quiet knowing that simply waits to be recognized. Prayer from the heart has a simplicity that the busy problem-solving mind often dismisses as too slow, too incomplete. The heart's response bypasses the head and speaks from essence—from your soulful connection to life.

Carl Jung, the Swiss psychiatrist, when delving into the beliefs of indigenous people was told that because white men think with their heads they are misled and troubled, while whole, healthy people think with their hearts. Heart's way is the way of deep centrality creating an affirmation of certainty and purpose. Confirmation. A reason to be. This centering, believers say, is a natural intention of the heart. They are dismayed to see anyone live otherwise. To do so is to alienate yourself from your own true nature.

Time seldom erases the essential truths of Nature. True, they may be obscured by new belief systems, distorted by changes in attitude, or proclaimed so dangerous that they are removed from the literature. Still the resonance of the heart will not be silenced. The wisdom remains, forging with each and every beat the human connection to the spiritual pulse that infuses life with meaning, that teaches us to be of good heart. Such is *Ab*'s featherweight of truth that may or may not tip the scales of judgment when ignored. No matter, the Tantric dance of the universe continues to be reenacted by the heart's beat. The sacrifice of the still-beating heart to the gods of ancient

Meso-America has blended with the Sacred Heart of Christianity, and now today is teaching us anew as science is able to transplant a donor heart into the breast of another host.

Heart to heart we are linked by a code so primordial it defies explanation: so elegant in its wisdom the most exquisite of catechisms pale by comparison.

The Steady Beat of the Heart

In Egyptian lore, the *Ab* appears also as a link between the heart and soul in its depiction as carrier of the "blood soul" that is said to emanate from the mother's heart energy through the umbilical cord to the fetus. This link was credited with maintaining a soulful connection for the unborn child as precursor to the development of the child's own unique soul with birth. The belief appears to have originated with the Egyptians, who believed that the child was formed from the maternal menstrual blood.

In truth, the quiet steady *drum-thrum* of the maternal heartbeat lends the fetus, from conception, an essential nonverbal message of ancient origin and life-sustaining reassurance whose traces remain within the cellular memory of the body for a lifetime. This beat is every human fetus's first link with its own humanity, encoded deeply within its cellular memory. Even today energy workers have found this concept meaningful in their work with cardiac patients. Julie Mott, in her work with therapeutic touch during cardiac surgeries, has noted that this earliest encoding of maternal heart energy can be drawn upon as a resource to steady the heart of the patient during periods of high stress or vulnerability. Apparently, as difficult as it may be for our scientific and "rational" mind to understand, there is evidence that the cellular memory of the prenatal maternal relationship is encoded in the complex neuronal web of the heart's memory system and can be reactivated by positive touch or meditation or imaging, encouraging the patient to hang on—to take heart—that all will be well. No one is alive and without this echo—this "code of life." Which is why you'll read in chapter 3 about the heartful importance of finding some sincere connection to the one who mothered you, so you can love yourself and others with a clear heart.

Ab shines out from ancient Egyptian hieroglyphics imaged as a dancer, a precursor to the growing awareness that every cell in our body is in fact in a vibratory dance with the universe. To dance soulfully is to join in the wheeling of the cosmos, the pulse beat of the planet, the heartbeat of the universe. One of the first drumming rhythms taught the novice drummer is the one-two beat of the heart. I was once part of a large group when the energy began to get out of hand. At first merely noisy and disjointed, it became increasingly frenetic and eventually developed a dangerous chaotic quality. A participant picked up a frame drum and began the slow, steady universal beat of the heart, and one by one others joined in the dance until we were aligned once more. At a neuronal level the heart and brain become entrained, linked rhythmically. That familiar beat sends a dual signal to both the banging heart and the busy brain. One angry thought can cause the heart to race, while a single loving thought can soothe us.

Heartbeat, the essence of your heart's rhythm, has woven itself inextricably throughout our language, keeping modern humankind unconsciously linked to the enduring wisdom embedded in many of the mystical beliefs of the past and undergirding a number of scientific discoveries in the present. Arising from an inexplicable sense that there is a source of deity within that sustains and guides us, we too cannot help but be strongly influenced. Unconsciously we are drawn by our connection to a relatively unexplored and unrecognized lineage whose history is recorded within the energetic memory of our heart.

The physiological truth is we are incarnately connected from conception to the heartbeat of our mother, who in her turn is linked to the heartbeat of her mother, ad infinitum. This human rhythmical force is electromagnetically linked to the heart pulse of Nature and ever deepening into the rhythmic rise and fall of the dancing pulse beat of eternity. *Life itself is full of heart.*

Itzhak Bentov in his rare gem, *Stalking the Wild Pendulum,* takes us step by step into the complex reality of what it is to be human. We are, he writes, energy—pure energy—pulsing cell to cell in a most remarkable way. Our cells "dance" with a vibrational off-and-on rhythm (called an oscillation) that is in synch with the vibrational patterns of the Earth. There is good reason that this is so. All matter is made up of atoms, and atoms have orbiting electrons that create a vibrational pulse. Our body mirrors the Universe. As the planets orbit the sun, so do the electrons orbit the nuclei of the atoms in every cell of your body. This constant motion of all matter, not just your body, is both solid matter that you can see and feel and energy fields that can only be seen and measured by machines. Just as your body pulses with the rise and fall of energy, this continuous electromagnetic rise and fall joins that of our planet and is met in response by the entire solar system and further, by the galaxy and further still, into infinity. Bentov says, "The universe and all matter is consciousness in the process of developing." Therefore, a dream or a symptom or a thought or a feeling is a form of consciousness that is developing—carrying a special developmental meaning for your body, your mind, or your soul. How often have we read of the central significance the cycles of the moon holds in the rituals and myths of the Nature-centered cultures, sensing that those rituals of yore were profoundly akin to the internal cycles of humanity—that they had less to do with ritual drama and far more to demonstrate about the intimate pulsing bond between Nature and human nature?

Bentov tells us that the pulse of the planet oscillates at about 7.5 cycles per second, as does the micro-motion (the cellular pulse) of your body. There are other louder and slower pulses carried by the organs of your body, but the pulsing of the cells make up the micro (smallest level) pulse. This subtle but pervasive body motion aligns you with the beat of this planet. Nature rituals, outdoor activities, toning, the electromagnetic surround of water, the vibrational interaction of consciously breathing with the environment—each evokes a poignant relief, an embodied sense of the seamless relationship among our personal body, our bit of incarnated matter, and the great *Mater* of Nature. The words *matter, matrix,* and *mother (Mater)* all come from the Latin *Materia,* which means "substance." Our heart beats as Hers. Our heart is rhythmically attuned to the exquisitely balanced pulsing in the dance of this Earth and our Universe—the most primordial of substance.

Heart and Soul

The intimate relationship between heart and soul is too historically evident to ignore. During the Middle Ages, kings would arrange for their bodies to be buried in one place and their hearts in another. Since the heart was believed to be the seat of the ultimate mystery— of the soul—strenuous efforts were made to prevent its desecration. It was anticipated that if the king's bones were ever disturbed, his soul, buried with the heart in a distant place, would be protected. This belief is not at all far-fetched when we are told that contemporary research into energy cardiology is once again placing emphasis upon the heart as the "orchestrator" of the life force, more powerfully influential than the brain on how we value ourselves and our relationship to others. One of the continuing mysteries of the human life force has been the role the heart plays in the ebb and flow of loving feelings. The effect that the absence or presence of love has upon an individual's life force cannot be overestimated as we increasingly recognize that love itself has a strong transpersonal source that makes life worth living even under the most dire of circumstances. *The heart is love's mediator and evocateur.*

Sadly, a life rhythmically in synch with the pulse of Nature is rare in today's frenetic flow. The discordant vibrations of contemporary life affect our heart's rhythm so forcefully we can feel torn apart as our natural rhythms shift. Breath, sound, and heartbeat are inextricably interwoven, creating part of the fabric of information that tells us how we are doing in the world. Undisturbed, our natural rhythms ebb and flow according to our nature. When we are jolted by an alien interference, we become aware, sometimes painfully, of how precious that natural ebb and flow is to our sense of ease, of identity and well-being. If the intrusion is too jarring, it can displace our connection to soul and we can feel "beside ourself"—thrust out of embodiment and lost. It may seem when such a situation is prolonged or intensified that our psychology suffers the most. In actuality our heart carries a major portion of the stress, often quietly, until it becomes too much to bear. As we face an ever-shrinking vitality or spirit for life we also have an ever-increasingly taxed heart. The cost is great because it depersonalizes us, separating us from our sensibilities and cutting us off from soulful participation in the web of life.

As humankind has become increasingly alienated from Nature-centered life, there have been entire communities dedicated to maintaining a rhythmic link with Universal Soul. In monasteries around the globe, continuous prayer chants are offered in the belief that one community can do the work for many. In recognition of the web of life that links all of humanity with all of Nature, the universal chant of *Aom* is a way, alone or in community, of connecting the personal heartbeat with the beat of the Infinite. As the *Ahh, Ohhh, Mmm* is formed within one's mouth, the procession of movement and vibration is a profound embodied teaching exercise. The *Ahh* begins at the back of the throat, followed by the *Ohhh* as its resonances fill the entire mouth, and the *Mmm* causes the lips to close, creating the embodied unity within. There is a fourth element, the silence that begins and ends the toning. The silence is the Ineffable presence of that which gives and holds and releases—the presence of the cosmic

Other. The divinity within matter—the mystery that resides within our very cells—is vibrationally present always through the sound, the influx and exhale of breath, the expansion and contraction of the embodied heart and within each pause between. Through the breath Spirit enters matter and we are *inspirited,* ensouled. As we become increasingly aware of the presence of the unfathomable vitality that is guiding us, mentoring us, sustaining us, our hearts become the source ground from which we can access the universality of our relatedness. Listening to the intuitive directions from the heart we feel less alone and more connected to life—and more accepting of death. Inevitably, gratitude and appreciation for life and all its mysteries emerges, forming an unspoken but deeply felt embodied personal mantra for healing and wholeness.

Heart and Health

Today modern humankind has to face another heart-related reality. It is well known that if we feel trapped in a futile and unsatisfying life we are susceptible to heart attacks and heart disease. Spiritually we have lost our heart for the life we have to lead. The stress that is inevitable when faced with an unsatisfying and inescapable job or relationship affects the balanced rhythms of the heart, and it "breaks." Cut off from the natural intuitive intelligence of the heart by stress and external intrusions, it is no wonder that our thoughts get jumbled and we feel trapped. Such an environment, both internally and externally, leaves us feeling depleted and toxic, short of breath and vigilant, lest we become further depleted, angry, and discouraged.

Judith Harris, Jungian analyst and author, reminded me that Rabbi Abraham Joshua Heschel describes the effect of this abrupt rise and fall in vitality well when he says, "Body without a spirit is a corpse, and spirit without a body is a ghost." Today's world has sped up, and we are being spun at ever-increasing amplitudes of change and interchange. Over stressed, we are living a *dispirited* life.

Our vital connection to the web of life is at risk daily for snarls, kinks, and dropped threads.

We tend to think of the heart as immobile, stuck within the confines of the rib cage. Further, we believe this fist-sized "entity" is beating away on the left side of the body. In actuality the heart is located beneath the ribs and more toward the sternum or center point of the chest. Again, when we turn to the metaphors of the healing arts of other cultures, we realize the heart as solely an organ is less than the sum of its total activity and influence. If you study yoga or tai chi, for example, you quickly realize the heart's vitality is anchored by the *chi,* the energy center just below the navel. The flow of energy from the heart is "anchored" within the constant flow of energy from the chi. This energy is easily explored and understood by noting the ways in which it expresses from each level of the chakras, the seven energy centers running from the coccyx (tailbone) to the crown of the head. Working with the metaphors of these energy centers gives you an inner map with which to understand how your breath (spirit) and your heart (soulful knowing) are working in concert to create the incarnated intention of wholeness.

Conversely, we have to barter our health in order to sustain the kind of existence required of us when we are showered with the disruptive proliferation of stress-filled energy fields. Sadly, for most moderns wholeness is a rare concept. Saturated with the stress of trying to keep abreast of the pressures of modern life, we are dying prematurely. Daily we are *losing heart.* Seventy percent of all emergency room admissions are stress related. One way or the other our environmental acceleration affects us physically and, make no mistake, we are also affected spiritually and psychologically. Yet within each breast there beats an organ that is carefully harboring our deepest desires, recording our most profound yearnings, and reminding us of our true nature, beat by beat, if we have but the "ears" to listen. It cannot and will not lie to you. This embodied intelligent wisdom is a living, breathing internal ally. Free for the taking, its messages if ignored may cost you nothing less than everything. The dance of life is the dance of eternity, and this book is an invitation to get into the dance.

The Heart's Intelligence

Meditation, quiet introspection, "counting one's blessings"—each is a form of ritual that draws us into a closer relationship with our heart's intelligence. In the West these rituals are often done repetitiously and without soul: without the recognition that they are heart centered and carry the potential for deep healing and insight. Because our history has long been based upon the separation of mind, body, and soul, we have been resistant to delving too deeply into any practice that appears superstitious or unfounded. Instead, we rely upon our priests and ministers to tell us about the soul, our physicians to take care of our physical concerns, and we keep the unruly products of our inner life to ourselves unless we are one of the brave few who talk about fantasies, intuitions, dreams, precognitions, and body wisdom.

When Rene Descartes, the seventeenth-century philosopher, declared, "I think, therefore, I am," Western culture was propelled into a new era. The principles of the intellect became superior to all others, and the body wisdom of the past was deemed irrelevant or irrational. With his declaration, all knowing by faith alone was dismissed, relegating the wisdom of the body and the psyche, the deep insights of dreams, intuitions, and the imagination to the ash heap of the intellectual fire of reason and logical thought. Mind rules— body submits.

Today humankind is on a quest to rewrite what it means to be human. We have but to look at the subject matter of our best-selling books or our talk shows or even our medical research to realize that the old rules are so inadequate that we cannot use them to explain the evidence that the human spirit is vaster and more intelligent

than we ever dared to imagine. Slowly, but with sincere appreciation the miracle of science and the highly developed tools of tech-
nology, we are awakening to the reality that *we are less human beings
attempting to find the spiritual meaning of life and more spiritual beings
attempting to learn how to live within the limits of a human form.* As science and the human spirit are joining forces, we are getting strong
reinforcement for continuing research into the spiritual capacity to
heal, how the body relies upon soul for healing, and even more
recently, what an extraordinary influential guidance emanates from
the intelligent capacities of the heart.

The New Science of the Heart

Quantum physicists tell us that even the most chaotic patterns of
Nature have at their center a cohesive organizing pattern. When this
pattern is understood, one can begin to recognize the extraordinary
cohesive nature of the universe. And so it is with our heart. We can
be frantic, beside our rational self with fear or excitement, and when
we turn our attention to our heart we can feel the steadying effect
of its repetitious beating, calling us home.

The human body is exquisitely designed as a microcosm of the
macrocosm of the universe. Later in this book I will discuss the God
Spot in your brain, which when stimulated with thoughts of positive belief sends radiant *healing* energy throughout your entire brain
and consequently throughout your body. I will also share with you
the remarkable lessons from the experiences of some heart transplant recipients as they are introduced to a uniquely intimate nonverbal relationship with their donor heart. We will discuss and marvel
at the number of fantastic ways your nature—your body—helps you
learn how to be as fully embodied and ensouled, as human as you are
able and intended to be.

Our attraction to the heart is no accident. Body wisdom can't be
extinguished. In the sixteenth century, Teresa of Avila, a remarkably

intuitive soul searcher, envisioned the constant flow of energy from the heart, the circulatory system, long before modern science provided us with microscopes, x-rays, and other windows into the human body. Steeping herself in prayer and meditation, the deeper she related to God the deeper her visions took her into the incarnated soul's realm, the body. Today we have intricate machinery that measures the electromagnetic energy of your body, your heart included, creating pictures of this energy so the physician or researcher can better understand the bodymind, the cellular intelligence of your matter. When you go for an EKG or EEG or any of the higher tech scans now in everyday use, the pictures are energy readings, not structural photographs. Scientists are beginning to recognize that the heart's energies have a strong and radiant influence in how you live physically, emotionally, and spiritually. They know also that the physical must no longer be isolated from the psychological or the spiritual in the treatment of the entire person. We are having to relearn and respect the evidence that there is a strong and enduring wisdom that resides in each and every cell of the body and is most accessible to us via the *sixth* and *seventh* senses—via the languages of embodied intuition and heart's wisdom.

In the pages that follow I invite you to join in the shift in consciousness that has begun as science and spirituality are blending. Do your own soul searching, make your own discoveries, and then tell me what you find. I am certain when you approach your heart you will discover a depth and breadth of wisdom you have always yearned for, offering you a fount of vitality and a source of guidance you will feel blessed by.

Remember, I am not offering you some esoteric practice used only by mystics and magicians. I am inviting you to step into a deeper relationship with your own embodied soul—to delve into the untapped resources contained within your unlived life. And, at the same time you will gain a foundation of practical and very real information about the absolute wonder that is your body and its capacity for both physical and metaphysical wisdom. It is as the poet Blake writes in the *Marriage of Heaven and Hell:*

No bird soars too high if he soars with his own wings.

CHAPTER 3

Meeting Your Heart

There is a vitality, a life force, an energy, a quickening,
that is translated through you into action, and because
there is only one of you in all time, this expression is
unique and if you block it, it will never exist
through any other medium.
—MARTHA GRAHAM

This vitality, this life force, so influences our perceptions of our relationship with the world around us and the people in it that without even thinking about it we rely upon its availability. When we are feeling most vital, we also feel more physically and spiritually attuned to our heart. During these times we utilize feedback from our heart to describe our intimacies ("You are in my heart"), our vulnerabilities ("My heart is aching"), and even our practical decision making ("I know in my heart this is right"), mostly believing that these phrases are merely figures of speech. The truth is that this seldom recognized but very influential energy is so interwoven into our sense of self that we cannot talk about ourself without using it as a reference point. So when we say an event caused our "heart to break," or the news was a "heart stopper," a listener nods in empathy, without having to ask what we "really" mean. The language that has grown out of our energetic relationship with our heart may have an unspoken shared meaning, but it also has a profoundly personal meaning that is unique to you alone.

Do you know what your heart loves? How long has it been, if ever, since you have inquired into what your heart yearns for? When you are weeping and don't understand why, do you turn to your heart for direction? Have you allowed your heart to break in order to feel, deeply and honestly, the vibrant richness of your own compassion? At night, just before sleep, do you turn to your heart space and review the events of your day with love and gratitude, first and foremost? When you awaken in the middle of the night filled with dread or anxiety, have you dared to ask your heart what you are avoiding about your own destiny, your own passion, your truth?

These are all deep and probing questions. They are soul-searching questions, and each deserves an answer if you are to live your life fully embodied, deeply and completely comfortable within your own skin. Just for a moment, pause in your reading. Go and get a hand mirror and sit and look deeply into your own eyes. What do you see there? How well do you know the depth of possibility that lies behind your eyes? The eyes, say the ancients, are the windows onto the soul. Do you know much about your own essence—your own soul? Go back to the earlier list of questions and ask yourself any one of these while looking deeply and without assumption into your own eyes. Don't ignore or brush off what you find. Write the answer down. Read it. Reread it. Now go back to your mirror and ask those eyes if they understood what they were answering. If not, ask again and again until you can feel the familiarity of the answer in your belly.

Now, *now,* we are ready to begin.

Your heart will answer you if you look deeply within yourself and listen for the reply, but you must be willing to meet your heart on *its* terms, not those of your ego. Meeting your heart may not lead to the guidance and the answers that you want, but rather those that are spiritually correct for your soul's purpose. Authentic knowledge of your deepest self requires a strong and unfaltering heart connection—a capacity to love life and welcome Spirit so that you will be prepared when she comes forward at the end of your life to greet you, robed as death. We cannot live life fully if we barter with death. Moment by moment we die a bit. The particularly precious gift that we humans possess is the gift of being able to choose *consciously* how we live, so that each inevitable letting go or falling away will feel timely, seasonal, expedient, as a heart-centered life rhythm.

One of the ways you will get to meet your heart is through the use of the Heart Notes, a series of exercises throughout this book that allow you to develop a more intimate relationship with your heart's wisdom and intelligence. These notes are designed to prompt insight and reflection—to ask probing questions and allow for heart-searching answers.

You are your most intimate life companion. No matter where you go or what you do, you are there. The life force that inhabits you and radiates from your heart is yours to draw upon and lean into or to ignore and feel the loss. The question is, Do you have the heart for living your life as fully as you are able?

HEART NOTES

In the Beginning

You won't be able to answer this question until you turn your attention inward and meet your heart on its own terms—get to know yourself from your most heart-centered perspective. Intuitive inner knowing is one of your heart's more prolific languages. You listen to this language without even realizing it. This exercise will help you begin to appreciate its presence. Take your journal and your mirror and find a quiet private place to sit.

- Hold your right hand out—palm up and your fingers lightly curled. You will be looking into the same palm print that was first formed at twelve weeks in utero. On your palm there are deep lines etched before your birth that are said by the ancients to be a map of your destiny. There is a head line, a life line, and a heart line.

- Trust your inner knowing about your life line, and write down how old you will be when you die.

- Next, take your mirror and look intently into your own eyes and ask yourself, "Am I willing to live a heart-centered life until I die?"

- Now, if you take your hands and cup them over your ears you can hear the familiar rhythmical drumming that has been present within you since those first days of uterine development. See if you can go back in time to before your birth, when you first heard this beat. Write down any thoughts, images, or feelings that come to you.

Your cellular intuition is always speaking to you about what matters most to you. It does so via the rhythms of your body. These rhythms are absolutely reflective of how you think and feel about your life. They change responsively to your deepest and most private feelings and to your every mood. If you are willing to meet your heart on its terms, you will uncover the truth of your life and the heart-centered reason for much that you desire.

What's in a Heart?

Until the miracle of human heart transplant surgery, most modern opinion regarded the heart from a physiological perspective only. Its presence and purpose was defined simply as a muscular organ—an essential life-sustaining pump. The observable valves opening and closing, dynamically forcing gallons of blood throughout miles of the body's arteries, veins, and capillaries was more evident and under-standable than the heart's capacity to keep body and soul intimately related. It is true that when the heart ceases beating, life is suspended and death quickly follows; however, we must not forget that the soul cannot be extinguished.

Ironically, not unlike the Meso-Americans I spoke of in chapter 2, who believed that unless a sacrificial heart continued to beat in their hands as it was removed from the body all the strength and power would be lost, modern surgeons have saved many a life by opening a person's chest and massaging the heart back into its own steady beating with the surgeons' own hands. When a person stops breathing we use CPR—a combination of external massage and forced breathing that gives this muscle a second chance to keep life's blood flowing. All of this evidence reinforces that pumping blood is the heart's primary function. However, this view of the heart is monocular—narrow and limiting. Individuals whose hearts have ceased beating and have been declared medically dead when revived report arresting spiritual experiences that appear to continue in spite of the body's demise. Pulsing, as you will learn in this book, is not the only language your heart uses to communicate its knowledge, expe-rience, and influence.

The pulsing of your heart responds to your spiritual energies in a variety of quiet yet essential ways that are healing to your total system. Scientists call this "coherency." As Dr. Paul Pearsall puts it, "If you want to get a glimpse of how your whole body/heart/brain/mind system sounds when it works collectively, listen to a symphony." When the mind, body, and soul are all aligned (coherent), there is a synchronized wave pattern that can be seen by recording the rhythms of breath, blood pressure, and heart rate. For example, when you are tired or frightened or angry, the rhythm of your heart may be irregular, not at all in alignment with the rhythms of your breathing or your brain waves. If they were each recorded and compared with one another, you would see a pattern of mismatched spikes. These spikes are representative of the turmoil that is affecting you mentally, physically, and spiritually. But when your entire system is rhythmically aligned, as it is in meditation or when you are happy, those same patterns would be so alike that you could see immediately the coherence or alignment that is the natural rhythm of a relaxed healthy system responding in a unified way. Learning to be aware of and to eliminate those things in our daily life that create negativity is the first step in creating a more coherent heart-centered life.

The thoughts, beliefs, opinions, and attitudes that we hold within us affect our well-being in multiple ways. Some of these are healing, while others can be quite damaging. Many of the damaging influences are subtle, and when they are brought into a clearer and more conscious focus we realize they wreak their damage because they are seldom if ever our true beliefs. I call them *unexamined* truths. Because they are so familiar we never examine the basis for why we respond as we do. For example, if we are largely invested in pleasing, competing, acquiring, and adapting to external influences, instead of thoughtfully making heart-centered choices, we can create a discordance within—much like a physical static. When this discordance is present we are unable to maintain a sense of coherence—of internal unity—because in all likelihood we are acting counter to our heart's guidance. This static is especially disruptive if we are parroting beliefs and behaviors that we don't or can't truly agree with. We lose, or worse, we never consciously develop any embodied heartfelt feedback about our health, our emotional well-being, and our spiritual balance. With each disruption our temperature, respiration, and blood pressure, even our immune system is buffeted by each sensation of success or failure, as if that reality, no matter how daunting, how self-defeating, is the only truth about our options in life. Stress builds. Fueled by this static, its presence and the sensations that accompany it become a familiar part of life.

Actually this static is like an internal signal that diverts us from listening to our deeper self. For example, as a child you knew that you loved a certain kind of music. When you heard it you felt fed, nourished, happy. Then as you grew up your peers insisted that the popular genre was far cooler—more important, even if you didn't resonate with it as much. But to keep up, to be part of the crowd, you listened less to your music and more to the popular choices. Yes, you lost the familiar pleasure of your music, but it seemed a fair trade for popularity—unless you sincerely factor in the loss of the deeper core values of the music you loved. What we love is always teaching us about who we are from deep within, teaching us also to recognize and be protective of what causes our heart to sing and our soul to speak to us intuitively. Eventually, in order to belong—to allay the fears of your ego that you will be different, left out, or overlooked—your ego told you that the original experience was probably "kid stuff." Better to leave that behind. Yet when you happen to hear that old kid stuff you can feel the poignancy and yearning for another time, with all its precious uncontaminated memories. What you don't realize is that those memories are tissue-level memories. The soul resides within your cells. And its messages resonate throughout your body—touching the core of each energy center or chakra from your tailbone to your crown—with its message. Your heart and soul still yearn for your return to core values, that music, that nourishment. This return provides the stability of feeling securely anchored, with a coherent inner sense of balance and connection. If we form a pattern of regularly denying our inner guidance, we will feel displaced (not completely at home in our own skin) and inadequate to life's challenges and requirements. Yet when we yield and turn inward, we discover strength instead of inadequacy and knowing instead of doubt. We become at ease in our own body. "Our deepest fear," writes author Marianne

Williamson, "is not that we are inadequate. Our deepest fear is that we are powerful beyond measure. It is our light, not our darkness that most frightens us."

An Inner Resource

When our thoughts, beliefs, opinions, and attitudes are inner sourced—when they arise out of soul-searching and intimate self-inquiry—we begin to feel in unison with a strong inner sense of who we are and how we wish to live life. Turning to our heart in order to connect with a more spiritual self, we discover an inner resource that is more intense and more loving than anything or anyone we have ever known. The soul-filled experiences of the poets and mystics begin to make personal sense. When we read the poet Rumi as he writes, "In the body of the world, they say, there is a soul and you are that," we catch a glimpse or an intuition of the presence of the uniquely personal other that has been patiently waiting within.

We can feel a very different sort of energy emanating from our heart than from our belly or our brain. Something strong and exciting, challenging yet calming at the same time. Since most of us have always been outer directed—seeking the approval of others before we trust in ourself—we are timid, anxious, not knowing exactly if this feeling is okay, if it is acceptable. How to describe it? What to call it? Will church, friends, others approve? What about all the old messages against trusting myself?

Harvey, a participant in a group that meets weekly to learn how to listen to the body, said pensively one afternoon,

> It has taken me six years to get it. Every time I am around J. my heart does all sorts of crazy things. Sometimes I feel like I can't breathe, sometimes the banging of my heart against my chest wall feels like I have hoofbeats pounding away inside, sometimes I can feel my heart aching. At first I sexualized these feelings, pretty

well convinced that I was, if not in love, then into a heavy attraction. As things progressed I felt less and less at ease. Then I began to feel anxious, unhappy. I've told myself I'm being foolish—exaggerating—that I'm probably allergic to something—maybe her perfume or her aggravating messiness? Now I realize I am allergic! Allergic to how her presence negatively affects my heart's energy. I had to first believe in the old self-deprecating way that this heart thing was something I was doing—something about myself that is flawed or unreasonable and therefore can't be trusted. Little did I know that my body was telegraphing wisdom—caution—good advice. When I began to trust that my body can teach me about myself through a physical reaction just as clearly as my mind can teach me with a thought I began to realize that I have many ways to express my deepest and truest feelings. Then I knew that this relationship was not good for my heart. This makes my favorite saying, "Follow your gut" take on a whole new and deeper meaning. When your gut speaks it may be because you are not listening to your heart!

HEART NOTES

Removing Roadblocks to Trust

Place your journal and a hand mirror nearby. Ask yourself, "Are there ways I automatically discount my own wisdom?" Maybe you were told as a child, "You are so impulsive, you act before you think." Maybe you say to yourself, "I'm absolutely untrustworthy with money," or, "I can never figure out when someone is lying to me." Or you may carry a free-floating anxiety about your capacity to handle certain aspects of your life—like the feeling that you just can't say "No." Once again, take your journal and your mirror and find a quiet spot.

- Make a list of the ways in which you feel uncertain of yourself or ways in which you feel you can't trust yourself.

- After you have made your list, choose one of the items on it.

- Take your mirror and look deeply into your own eyes and ask your heart, "Is this a truth about me?"

- If the answer is "Yes," ask what you can do about making a change. Imagine that the answer is held within your heart. Go there, listen, and write down whatever you hear. Commit yourself to genuinely try the change. This is not a quick fix. All soulful change takes time, conscious commitment, and a willingness to believe in the outcome.

- If the answer is "No," then write a commitment to yourself that each and every time you find yourself using this reason to not trust yourself you will stop, turn to your heart, and ask for the courage to remove this roadblock.

The Heart That Knew Its Killer

Slowly evidence is growing to support the notion now proposed by energy cardiologists and heart transplant recipients that the heart is vastly more influential and involved in helping us grow spiritually than we ever gave it credit for. These pioneers on the cutting edge of cardiac research tell us that the heart is indeed a remarkably intelligent contributor to our well-being and to the roots of our integrity.

Today the reports of medical doctors and scientists sound familiar—reminiscent of the so-called anecdotes of mystics, intuitives, and folklore. If we allow ourselves to explore this new land of the heart with our inner vision and to listen to its communiqués with our inner ear, we may find that what we learn is never trivial or misleading. The evidence is arising from many sources these days, none more interesting or more mystifying than that of the heart transplant recipient.

Dr. Paul Pearsall is a psychoneuroimmunologist whose work with heart transplant recipients led him to write *The Heart's Code,* a collection of remarkable accounts of post-surgical experiences of people who have received the heart of another into their bodies. Each account of how the presence of the transplanted heart is experienced reveals a wisdom and intelligence that appears to emanate from the heart, not from the head. Some of the donor heart recipients, later called *cardio-sensitives* in an attempt to describe their receptivity to their transplanted hearts, report memories and sayings and insights that clearly belong to the donor, not the recipient. The accuracy of these experiences is too real to be ignored or explained away. Some recipients find themselves repeating an expression once favored by the donor, or having a food craving or even a dream that links them to the donor or the donor's history. As Dr. Pearsall gathered accounts of these incidents, he could not deny that in many there was a common thread. Each person felt a sense of spiritual change. This change was more than the obvious physical trauma or psychological recovery one would anticipate from such an operation. Maybe these insights are the response of an imagination trying to make sense of having its body's heart removed and the heart of another put in its place. Or, maybe the poets and mystics are right when they speak of the heart's deep knowing: that *"the heart has reason that reason alone doth not know."*

Speaking in Houston, Texas, about the role the human heart plays in our psychological and spiritual life, Dr. Pearsall called on a psychiatrist in the audience who volunteered a story about one of her cases that she felt was pertinent to his presentation. An eight-year-old girl had received the heart of a murdered ten-year-old. The patient began being terrorized at night with dreams of a man who was murdering a little girl. Her mother brought her into therapy because she felt these dreams revealed the identity of the donor's murderer. Together the mother and the psychiatrist agreed to contact the police. Fortified with the descriptions provided by the girl's dreams, the police found the murderer. The child knew the time, the weapon, and even the garments the killer wore from her dreams.

*Heart to heart—soul to soul—*for an instant in time the donor and her heart's new host were as one. No one could refute the fact that the eight-year-old knew nothing of the details of her heart donor's death, yet after receiving the heart her dreams drew her a vivid and accurate picture of the donor's last moments.

Other Stories

Dr. Pearsall began to collect these accounts from transplant recipients after his interest was inspired by his own life-threatening experience with cancer. These strange stories—clearly associated somehow with the donor more than with the host—have been reinforced by a dancer's experience after her heart-lung transplant. The dancer, Claire Silva, has written her story in her book, *A Change of Heart*.

After Claire's transplant she began to crave chicken nuggets of the fast-food variety. As a classical dancer she was accustomed to the strict discipline of diet and exercise that precluded such unlikely treats. Baffled, she told her surgeon about her craving, and it was his turn to be baffled. You see, her donor so enjoyed these nuggets that there was a half-eaten packet at the scene of the fatal accident that cost him his life and gave her an extension on hers.

What to make of such a strange occurrence? A coincidence? Maybe some sort of telepathy or even a conversation overheard while under anesthesia? Or has it taken this very unusual medical advance to highlight what has been present and available to us all along? Our culture has been vigorous in restricting credence about irrational or inexplicable communications. Yet we marvel at the "rare" circumstance when a scientist dreams the solution to a complex problem or a musician just "hears" a musical composition in its totality. We call it a miracle or a mystery or even a coincidence when the non-locality of a prayer or the act of laying on of hands heals, as if something unknown and unknowable is at work—something way beyond human understanding or explanation.

Isn't it possible that heart transplant recipients are giving us first-hand accounts of a concrete embodied experience—evidence that what has been accepted as mysterious or miraculous or even inexplicable may be inner sourced, and that our heart carries the strongest signal from this untapped inner resource?

At the time of Claire's transplant her experience was one-of-a-kind, so nothing could scientifically be ruled out. Claire was unshakable in her insistence that she felt the presence of this new heart in other ways, each very different from how she had experienced her own heart. For instance, when she told her surgeon that this new heart seemed to beat further back in her chest than her heart had, he confirmed her perceptions. Because the donor heart was larger than her original heart the surgeon had, in fact, had to place it further back in her chest cavity. On this point at least Claire's sensitive relationship to her new heart was reinforced as a physical fact. Claire realized that after the transplant "the center of my being does not feel fully mine." Further, she was sensing something she could only define as possibly aspects of the donor's spirit or personality.

There were other sensations. There persisted a sense of having to get used to a different rhythm, a different energy. "I had a definite sense that I was not alone," Claire writes, "and when I joined a transplant support group I found that I was not the first to have this feeling after transplant surgery." Thomas had received the heart of a New York teenager. He found himself using language he had never used before surgery, startling his wife with his swearing. The language was spontaneous and felt simultaneously appropriate and inappropriate. "Like me, and not me." Thomas is certain his heart came from an African American, because after surgery his former bigotry seemed to fade and he was drawn to black people socially. He began to feel deep empathy and anger at the plight of black people dying of starvation. This stance wasn't a conscious choice—it simply could not be denied.

Some reported that their new heart had a will of its own, resisting things that held interest and good energy for the recipient before the transplant. Some were distressed or amused because a pre-transplant interest in a hobby or skill or even a recreational pursuit was firmly erased or replaced by newer interests. These new preferences were relatively temporary. After the new heart and the host brain became entrained—energetically in synch with one another—the feelings began to diminish, but initially they were in such bold contrast to the recipient's usual tastes and behavior that they could not be ignored.

Each of these stories is evidence for what Dr. Pearsall calls the "heart's code," a personally unique relationship between the heart and its original body that is undeniably conveyed to the new host in a variety of forms—some through thoughts, some through taste, others through unfamiliar memories. When I first heard these curious, almost magical stories of the cellular capacity of the heart to remember its donor even after the heart has been transplanted into a new host, I felt a keen sense of recognition.

Life Inside of Life

Claire expressed that this new heart as "other" is not too unlike a woman's experience of pregnancy, particularly when the mother begins to sense that the fetus is developing an energy and a personality all its own. There is no rationale for this, just a strong innate sense of knowing. Nature has a way of taking care of the paradox of pregnancy. A fetus is totally dependent on and vulnerable to the mother, and this must be balanced by the uniqueness of the new life force growing within the uterus so that the mother knows, intuitively, that this life is both in her and not hers alone. Those who have an increased intimate relationship with their transplanted heart describe the bond in much the same way. They speak of a wisdom and a knowing that is "in me but not entirely of me."

Anyone who has ever been pregnant knows about this paradox. On the one hand there are two bodies breathing as one, and yet there is a distinctly different energy and strength forming within that both mother and fetus must independently grow accustomed to. Each, fetus and mother, is an extension of the other in mutual vulnerability and interdependence. Each is also separate and growing, with its own unique soulful energy and destiny. Many a pregnant woman, like many heart transplant recipients, has had dreams or thoughts about her unborn child that have pointed out both the distinct differences and the intimacy that is mutually shared via nonverbal communications between mother and "other."

Undeniable Connections

Frieda recounts a dream that she believes came to her to "ease her heart" about a very difficult pregnancy. She dreamed that the baby appeared as a small animal and thanked her for being his mother. The animal gave her a tiny plant she did not recognize and told her it would help her with her sorrow when she said "good-bye."

Frieda awakened knowing that she would not carry her pregnancy to full term. She lost her baby the following weekend. Later when she looked the plant up in her gardening book she was awed to read that it was called "bleeding heart." She felt her child had touched her heart and soul deliberately to help her understand that even in grief there is the promise of springtime and renewal. "I had, for the first time, a clearer sense that the child growing in my womb had a destiny all its own, that I was a partner in this mysterious process but not the final say," she wrote.

Frieda remembered:

> I grieved, railed against the impersonal forces of fate that would take my baby's life and I, no, my heart, ached and ached. Some days when I was particularly angry my heart would fill my chest with staccato jarring beats and I would become frightened and superstitious. I was afraid I had gone too far in my anger toward God

and I was going to be punished with a heart attack. Then one afternoon it was gray and pouring rain outside, the steady downpour matching my mood and my tears. I turned to my heart to ask if I was going to die too. Am I about to have a heart attack? I wondered. I sat and waited. The room began to recede. I felt quieter and calmer, then I realized I was watching an inner screen. The image was of a great vaulted room filled with soft light. I knew I had entered my own heart! Slowly it began to dawn on me that I could return here again and again until I felt healed. Those earlier hoof beats that scared me so were a summons to life, not death! So if anyone asks me I'll tell them I discovered that my heart is always dreaming the story of my life. Sometimes the images come at night while I am sleeping and sometimes they come when I am waiting deep within for a message, for guidance, from my soul. Since my baby's death I have the profound assurance that waking or sleeping I am never alone. My heart speaks for my soul and all I have to do is listen and learn from this ever-present blood tie.

The Maternal Blood Soul

Frieda's willingness to surrender to her grief, to listen and to learn what her heart knows about her deeper self because of *this ever-present blood tie* is reflective of the ancient Egyptian belief in the blood soul, the intimate nonverbal bond between a mother and her fetus as they share a single blood source and are linked soul to soul. Contemporary science tells us that the relationship begun between the fetus and the mother is so vitally influential after birth that the connection made between the heart of the prenate in utero, and the heart of the mother, must be immediately reestablished after delivery. If this energetic, nonverbal connection is irreparably broken during delivery or after birth, the child will suffer marked limits in its immediate ability to relate to and feel safe within the new environment. This is why conscious and aware physicians and midwives place the child on the breast of the mother as soon after delivery as possible. Joseph Chilton Pearce, physician and world-renowned author, reports that if this connection is made immediately after birth, "each heart (both that of the mother and the child) sends a signal to its brain and the brain shifts its functioning accordingly, and a bond is established in the new environment, giving an underlying unity to the new diversity." Nature responds to the need of a human infant to have its own individualized experiences by utilizing the innate wisdom of the heart. While still deeply connected with the familiar life-sustaining security of the energetic field of the maternal heart, the infant heart has a stabilizing opportunity to reorient itself to the new relationship with its own brain. Human birth is all about incarnation, about spirit in matter. Soul to soul we are vibrationally linked in nonverbal cellular memory and blood ties to the one who gives birth to our body, whether our literal experience of our biological mother has been loving and intimate or not. To ignore what we do ourselves by hating our origins, or feeling unmothered or motherless will cut us off from a richly connected source of embodied energy. It is as if we have welded shut the access to the realm of the maternal—of *Mater*—of matter—of Mattering. If you truly wish to meet your heart, you have to be willing to receive its wisdom about what matters in your most private thoughts and feelings.

Mattering: The Cellular Feminine

For a woman this connective vibration is recorded not only in her emotions and her dreams but cellularly, in her mitochondrialDNA (mDNA) as well. This bit of genetic material that resides within each cell like a solar power pack, energetically keeping the cell vibrantly active, is passed from mother to daughter as a biological genealogical record. Sons receive this maternal genetic material also, but they are unable to pass it on to their progeny, so this uninterrupted historical cellular inheritance is particular to females. No matter how concrete, how pragmatically you live your life, if you are reading this book you and I know that you are beginning to question what is missing. Eventually each woman, if she wishes to know who she is in her heart of hearts and what her life is all about, will ask what it means to know that her body carries a record of maternal blood bonds within every cell linking her without refute to first woman, first mother, first daughter, first birth, first body record of incarnation. Equally, every man can join the woman he is connected to in their shared experiences of listening to the heart's intelligence, knowing that her womanly body may respond to the experience differently but they both are delving into the mystery of soulful embodiment—of conscious interaction with a wisdom greater than that of the head alone.

For now, it is important to know that if you cannot remember a single redeeming connection to your own mother, you can rest assured that in the womb you were being touched also by the long motherline that preceded your conception—grandmother, great-grandmother, great-great-grandmother. . . . Again, the metaphors of the feminine remind us that male or female, the body is the soul's human container: its womb, its mother, its matter, *Mater.*

By placing the newborn in the crook of the left arm, close to the heart, no matter which arm is the dominant one, instinctually the entire soul-filled body yields to that ancient birthing rite of welcome. The mother's heartbeat is the first touchstone of soulful embodiment for the newborn. This ritual reconnection to the heartbeat of the mother is no empty or accidental ritual. This earliest of heart sounds affirms that the new soul will not be without a mentor while in this body, and further it lays down the reinforcing memory that will eventually sustain the body as death approaches. In the end we all approach death as a singularly personal journey companioned by whatever we have held in our hearts as our deepest and most resolute truth. Dying can be yet another step of loving the body that has been your soul's home, serving your soul so faithfully, or it can be a disembodied experience of refusal to accept the inevitable, fearing that you will be as "homeless" in death as you have been in life. As you deepen your relationship with your heart's intelligence, you cannot avoid discovering the depth of love that emanates from it moment by moment. This love is revitalizing and will provide you with the profound experience of rebirth into the family of humankind, helping you to see that loss, aging, and death are natural cycles in your soul's growth. Our body comes from the stuff of this planet—from matter—and to matter we return, but the energies of your soul are eternal. Linking the natural evolution of birth, death, and rebirth, the *Book of the Dead* offers prayers for rebirth to "heart of my mother." Imagine—a prayer for safe journey from the crook of the earthly mother's arm at birth to the curved cradling of the Universal Mother, of the Earth, of matter, at death.

Many of us grow up feeling the terrible loss of never having been mothered. For some of us it's a physical reality and for many more it is an emotional or psychological loss. Without a conscious remembrance of some molecule of heart connection to the one who mothered you, your soul will feel cut off from her embodied source ground—ungrounded and alone.

It is not some passing fad that modern men and women alike are searching for a meaningful relationship with the Goddess—with the archetypal feminine. Culturally we have been taught from earliest memory that we get in touch with our feelings, rediscover our capacity for nurture and our deep hunger to give and receive love via our capacity to access the energies of the feminine. We can and do learn how to awaken this capacity within ourself from either parent. If however, we receive it from the mother, the continuity between the visceral in utero connection and the physical self after birth remains unbroken, establishing a heart-centered embodied sense of relational security. This embodied sense is the foundation for an unquestioned trust in the nonverbal messages and signals from our sixth and seventh senses, from our intuition and our heart's intelligence. If we receive this capacity from the father because the mother is absent after birth, we have a kind of gap, a break in continuity, between our in utero sense of secure relationship and our intellectual sense of being seen and feeling well received, accepted. This has nothing to do with whether or not a man can be as nurturing with a newborn as a woman. This is about Nature and how the body of a neonate is attuned to the body of the womb in which it was formed. So when the mother is absent, the infant body has to readjust itself after making a huge adjustment from the internal environment of the mother to the external one without her. According to Dr. Pearce, if the nonverbal connection between fetal and maternal heart is broken, a confusion is created in the body of the newborn so that she cannot adapt to this new environment and feel comfortable in her own body. *If you are not at home in your own body, you cannot be at peace with your life or yourself.*

The disruption creates a psychospiritual ambiance of alienation in which you question your sanity at times because you *feel* like an alien. Psychoculturally, the disruption creates a condition of marginality that leaves you feeling on the outside of life—a participant, yes, but without fully embodied membership. Thus separated from any visceral heart-centered sense of trust in Nature, of Great Mother, we are separated also from the roots of our own nature. We doubt our inner signals, doubt our uniqueness, yet we long to be different. But without any memory of being securely held and fully accepted just as we are, we are afraid to be different. And we are drawn to any story, myth, or ritual that evokes even a tiny fragment of our lost connection. Hence, the search for the Goddess. The archetypal energies of the Goddess carry hope for a reconnection to the blood soul of the mother. A search for a visceral blessing. No human alive truly wishes to feel unmothered. In spite of this many are repulsed by the memory of the one who mothered them. Recalling Martha Graham's words at the opening of the chapter, the unique vitality that is yours alone and first established through the heart-to-heart connection in utero has to be honored and consciously cultivated in order for you to freely and confidently claim your unique quickening—your heart's vitality that translates into your energy, your life lived fully and with a sense of purpose.

Many of us were born to mothers and fathers who simply didn't, or couldn't, give us any embodied affirmation of the vitality we brought with us from the womb. Almost immediately after delivery we sensed the numbing distance between ourself and all that we had learned to rely upon as we measured our security and our reason for being.

Finding your way back to the heart's vitality in order to live fully within your body can be done symbolically. In today's culture we confuse the biological mother and what she has or hasn't given us with the inner feminine and what we can or cannot retrieve. We search for elders and reject them if they don't deliver. We chose partners covertly hoping that they will provide us with the nurture we missed out on as children. We have grasped at the concept of a mentor, hoping that this will glean us some fair share of the maternal blessing we reject as adults but yearn for in our hearts. We neither need nor want the romanticized, infantalizing mama who replaces our good sense and independence. What we do seek is an inner sense of blessing, a sense of having a visceral feedback loop from an older, wiser woman's words to our heart that keeps us soundly and securely in touch with our own intuitive sense of embodied security, no matter how different or distant we become.

HEART NOTES

Recovering the Blood Bond

This exercise will allow you to recover a sense of that original in utero experience of unconditional acceptance and love that is central to strengthening your relationship to your heart's loving intelligence.

- Find a quiet and private spot where you can be alone with your thoughts. Turn off your telephone. Some like to play soft music while they do this exercise. If you do, please play something that will not distract you. You will want to have your hand mirror, your journal, and art materials nearby. If you have a picture of yourself as a baby or young child, place it here beside you along with a cup or glass of milk, a piece of bread, and a dish of honey.

- Before you begin, write this pledge to yourself in your journal and then speak it aloud while looking into your own eyes in the hand mirror. Be very aware of exactly how you feel about such a commitment.

> I,_____, promise myself to be open and receptive to allowing the memory of a single irrefutable moment of absolute acceptance from my mother (or the one who mothered me) to come into my consciousness. I believe this memory is waiting to be recalled, stored within my heart and recorded deep within my heart's memory. When I remember I promise myself that this will be all I will need to reawaken my unique connection to the loving intentions of my heart and soul. I make this pledge to myself.

- After you have made and signed your commitment, turn your attention inward and go back to the earliest memory you have of feeling seen and appreciated by your mother or the one who mothered you. This can be a grandmother, a nanny, an older sister, a neighbor. Set aside the "yes, buts." Your heart is leading you to a deeply embedded truth that must be reaffirmed according to the nature of your life—not according to an ideal cultural image. Cry if you feel tears, shout, argue—be involved with this journey! Set all judgments aside! You may have to dismantle years of thoughts, anger, and debris. Stay with your heart's direction. If you feel lost, turn to your heart and ask that this vital and enduring embodied wisdom show you the image or the impulse that you are seeking.

- If you can only uncover a tiny feeling, a brief memory, do not reject it. You have what you are looking for. Remember every detail and refuse to diminish it one iota. Go back and read your pledge and then go to your journal and write down in detail what you remembered.

- Now create some conscious ritual of acceptance and embodiment of the reawakening of your heart. I suggest you use the milk, bread, and honey, as they are the symbolic foods of the feminine, the fruits of Nature. It is your original nature always to be in tune with the wisdom and loving intelligence of your heart.

Creating a ritual that allows you to reflect more deeply and specifically upon your experience with the Heart Notes will reinforce your capacity to celebrate how well you know your own uniqueness. All too often we join in the rituals created by others and miss the rich expressions of our own imagination. When a ritual arises from your experience, it becomes memorable and will feed you long after the exercise has been completed.

CHAPTER 4

What Your Heart Knows

Something in us, no matter how much we flee it,
summons us. We may avoid it all our lives,
but deep down, something knows.
—JAMES HOLLIS

Long before your brain has sorted something out, your heart simply knows. And why would this be so? Tor Norretranders in his book, *The User Illusion: Cutting Consciousness Down to Size,* tells us that it is our senses, not just our brain, that are absorbing more than 11 million bits of information about our place in the universe per second. Your ego can only make conscious use of fewer than twenty-one of these bits each second. The remainder are stored within your body's unique form of energy intelligence that is called your *bodymind*. These bits of information are contained in your very cells as patterns of energy and emotions. They carry information about the universe you live in. All these bits are sorted rather generally in categories that we call emotional, physical, affectual, and so on, to be retrieved if and when they are needed. When these stored impressions reemerge as images we call them insights or hunches or dreams. And when they emerge as body sensations we usually call them symptoms. Because our culture is accustomed to dividing experience into rational or irrational categories, we have learned to bypass the less easily defined experiences brought to us by our body functions. We may ignore or neglect these sincere messages about the state we are in, or need to be in, but our frequent use of symbolic language ("That made my hair stand up on the back of my neck," or "My heart turned to stone, or to ice," or even, "My heart sang") to describe our relationship to these messages betrays our indifference. Your soul, the essence of you, utilizes the sensations of its body, your matter, to speak its plain unvarnished truths to you. Are you listening?

The intelligence contained in each cell of your body is a marvel. First, each and every cell contains the chemical mapping of your DNA. This bit of cellular matter maps exactly the pattern and structure of your creation. Each cell has in its matter an *exact hologram* of your total being. The principle of a hologram is that any fragment of the holographic pattern contains a replica of the total pattern. Hence your primary DNA pattern—the chemical blueprint that determines in utero how your body will be formed—is replicated in every cell in your body.

These patterns are not concrete. They are composed of energy frequencies that fluctuate in accord not only with your body's specific needs but also in conjunction with the electromagnetic pulsing of the universe. In other words, each and every cell of your body is *always* interacting with both the personal you (your body) and the universal you (as a part of all of Nature). When you feel especially centered and say you are in "the flow," what you are feeling is a deep body response to the presence of your balanced intimate relationship with the pulsing of the universe—with Spirit—or God. So if you have ever wondered how real—how valid—the concepts of soul in matter or being one with Nature really are—*they are as real as your consciousness about your own cellular composition.*

The HeartMath Institute of Boulder Creek, California, is doing extraordinary focused research into a single aspect of this relationship: the capacity of human matter to activate and radiate the healing energies of love. This research has led to much of the information we now have concerning the electromagnetic influence of the heart's energies.

In the 1980s I participated in an activity called Hands Across America. In this project people from coast to coast were asked to form an unbroken chain of clasped hands from East to West without prejudice or judgment. My husband and I flew out to California to participate in the final link as this energy reached its end destination. The sense of unity and shared human experience was palpable, and many stories of a change in attitude or perspective followed. The single most repeated emotion was one of opening the heart and feeling connected by love. Not sentimental love, not genital love, but heart-centered empathy for all of humanity. Each person who participated became a holographic carrier of the total energy of universal connection—of the holograph of universal DNA that is the master pattern of relational wholeness.

Of all the organs in your body, your heart is proving to be one of the clearest and strongest voices for your soul. It is a most remarkable organ. The heart alone contains over 1 million neurons, each capable of receiving and sending information throughout your biochemical communication network. Because of its power and its centrality to the functioning of your entire body, your heart's reaction to your deepest and most private feelings is immediately influential upon your entire system. This influence can be thought of as messages from your heart's wisdom or knowing. Your heart's knowing will be quite different from that of your head, since your heart is distilling every experience down to what is essential for your well-being, not what is pleasing to others or what is merely good enough to get by. The language of your heart is to be felt, not heard—to be experienced, not spelled out. The wisdom of your heart is much like the wisdom that comes from your dreams. You may miss it at first glance, but as you become more intimately involved its message speaks to you. Your soul is always teaching you and speaking to you in its special symbolic way—teaching you about your purpose in life, showing you your own spiritual resources.

Knowing What We Don't Know That We Know

In learning to trust the wisdom of your heart it is always helpful to listen for and respect the other ways your soul is speaking to you. The more you learn to trust the uniqueness of your inner world, the more trusting you will become of the guidance you find emanating from your intuition, your feelings, your dreams, and your body sensations.

For several decades now I have recorded my own dreams and listened to recollections of the dreams of hundreds of other people. Over and over again I am privileged to assist dreamers in clarifying and following the wisdom and direction of their dreams. I have had the distinct experience of dreaming a dream clearly intended for someone else. I have also had the experience of dreaming a dream about someone else, and when I shared it with that person they heard a significant piece of insight with meaning for him or her alone. Dreams often speak a truth from the heart, as Frieda's dream of her unborn child did for her in chapter 3. Dreams are not mysterious mystical curiosities. Dreams are a natural human experience. The imagistic language of your dreams appears mysterious because it is seldom concrete; instead it is symbolic and full of metaphoric meaning. Dreaming is one of the most natural things we do to access the untapped reservoir of knowledge we contain. As long as dreams are treated like rare and often scary messages from elsewhere—out there, beyond—the profoundly intimate dialogue that is taking place between your psyche and your knowing heart is shut off from your own good sense.

Dreaming is just one way you process the less accessible, subtle level of information that assists you in knowing what you had no idea you knew. You can approach your dreams as magical and mystical—as an inexplicable gift—or a curse if they are nightmares. In actuality the mysterious source is within you—your essential self. When you are dreaming you are telling yourself something that you have taken in but are not consciously aware of yet. From that quiet but steady source of knowing that speaks to you about your authentic being, images are drawn just for you, nightly. Equally, your heart communicates with you about your authentic feelings and your capacity for loving yourself and others that your waking experience either is unaware of or has never fully explored.

Conversations with Yourself

Awake or asleep, you are always having an ongoing unspoken conversation with your inner self. When these conversations get stalled or remain unfinished, your dreaming self then paints you a picture that is metaphoric. In other words, the dream image, just like many of our symptoms and emotions, is full of meaning that can only be discerned as you make associations to it. The symbolic meaning of an image or a symptom will be distorted if you take it literally. For example: I dream my best friend hates me. If I literalize this symbolic message I will believe she must really hate me. But your dream wants you to recognize that part of yourself that is most like your friend and is causing you to treat yourself hatefully. Everything in a dream is about an inner energy in yourself. And every message from your heart is about how you are responding to your world—both inner and outer. Your soul wants you to turn to your inner wisdom and make associations about what matters most in your life—right here, right now.

Suppose you dream of a chipped cup. When you associate to it, you muse that it reminds you of a cup you owned when you had your first apartment. Then you might wonder about *what in my life, or experience, got* chipped *while I lived in my first apartment? Or, what about me was* chipped *away?* Before you realize it, the chipped cup image is opening a door on feelings and possibilities that your waking self has overlooked or denied. In this exact same manner, suppose you realize that you frequently feel ill or uneasy in a certain situation. If you turn to your heart and make associations to the experience, you'll find how you are ignoring your inner wisdom about the situation and therefore are making yourself ill.

Hank had wanted a racy red convertible ever since he began to drive. Finally, at age thirty-six, he got a promotion, a raise, and the red car. At first he was excited to show it off and was deeply pleased with his new car. Then he began to notice that every time he got in it to drive home at night he felt his legs and face itching and a curious tightening of his shoulders that became painful to the touch. At first he ignored the symptoms. Then talking it over with a friend he convinced himself he was allergic to the upholstery—but why wasn't every part of his body that came in contact with the upholstery itching? So he ruled that out. For weeks he had various possibilities checked out, and then one day he realized these symptoms never seemed to appear in the morning on his way to work. A colleague, laughing, asked him if going home caused him to itch. Hank felt his shoulders knot up.

> This was such a weird, but absolutely undeniable replication of the symptom I had been trying to figure out that I was shocked. I kept my mouth shut because I didn't want to sound like a hypochondriac. When I went home I sat down and thought

about my relationship to this red car and I began to itch. It was subtle but very, very real. At first I wanted to deny what was happening—I felt like I was making it up. And then an even stranger thing happened: the tightness in my shoulders moved into my chest and I began to cry. I felt frightened, out of control—a grown man crying—and for what? As I sat torn between trying to stop the process and being equally amazed by it I had a memory of how heavily I drank in college. So much that I was thrown out of my fraternity and humiliated by my parents. I barely managed to stay in school because I felt so ashamed. The pain shifted to my heart, and I then realized that in my defiance back then I told myself that one day I would be *somebody,* I'd make lots of money and buy a red convertible that would make everyone envious of *me.* The next day I took my red car out for one last drive, sold it, and I still feel awed by what my heart revealed to me once I stopped trying to turn my feelings into a physical symptom that had to be cured. The entire experience felt like a waking dream where things seem real but somehow you know that they are not exactly real.

Hank's last statement is truer than he thinks. Your body is always dreaming. By this I mean your body has a rich symbolic existence that assembles all the sensations and experiences that your conscious mind is ignoring, and then, instead of drawing you a picture as your dreaming psyche does, it offers you a symptom or a spontaneous craving or a flood of tears that has a depth of meaning that goes far beyond the limits of the literal "picture." Your soul speaks using the symbolic representations that are always distilled right down to the essential meaning you need in order to live a heart-centered, balanced, soulful life. These meanings are easily accessed when you turn to your heart's wisdom.

Soul's Languages: The Metaphor
of Dreams, the Emotions of the Heart

Remember, your soul takes all those millions of bits of feelings and sensing and thoughts and insights and warnings, ad infinitum, that you have passed over and distills them down to what is most essential in your life, *right here, right now.* Your nighttime dream state and your heart's knowing are far more intimately engaged in your authentic life than you can imagine.

For instance, at night when you are sleeping, did you know that more of your brain is awake than when you are conscious? And as your sleeping mind creates the images and the scenarios of a dream from your deeper unexpressed wisdom, even though all of your actual muscle movements are inhibited, the neurons of your body fire in concert with the images of your dream. Dreaming is an *embodied* experience. It is a conversation that engages your entire self. If, in your dream, you are running from a fierce predator your heart will respond with racing, your breathing will increase to keep up, and the neurons of your legs will fire as if you are fleeing—even though you would appear to be inactive to anyone who might be observing you. You are an actively involved participant in this *symbolic* story about something essential that is yours alone to decipher and make meaning of. A dream is a total integrative experience. Your body, although apparently quiescent, is actively engaged at a neuron level. Your mind is engaged not only with the recall of certain memories but also with recreating the story of the symbolic event when you remember it the following day. Your soul is touching into your cellular memory and awakening a connection between your heart and your brain with the symbolic meaning of your dream. This meaning allows you to *feel* in accordance with both what you think and what you feel as a result of the dream. It is this sense of being fully engaged that makes dream recall so appealing to those who follow their dreams. When the insight gleaned from a dream feels correct to the dreamer it is a holistic experience, joining the mind, the physical body, and the sense of self, or soul. It does not take long to recognize that the symbolic information from any dream is made accessible to you at a time in your life when, if you listen to its wisdom, it can deepen your relationship to your sense of a personal indwelling guidance. Even if your cognitive mind forgets the dream with the first ray of sunlight or the first jangle of an alarm clock, your heart will have registered the essential emotional message of the dream on a cellular level. It is these two great body organs, your heart and your brain, working in concert that orchestrate the embodied context of your life. When what you feel and what you think are in accordance, you feel centered, confident, and whole. And, above all else, research continues to show us that your heart can survive without your brain, but the reverse is not so. Consequently, it appears that your heart can carry cellular memories of what is essential in your life even after it is transplanted in another person's chest.

Creating Life's Context

We are taught to give credence to our first five senses. Relying upon touch, taste, smell, sight, and hearing to define our world—both inner and outer—we also learn to be suspect of any other information, not realizing that we are also in constant communication with a non-tangible vibrational life force. This life force is far more internal than external. It resides in the depths of our soul—in every cell of our matter—in the caves and caverns of our heart. This life force, which Asians call *chi,* physicists call electromagnetic energy, and the religious call Spirit, is always knocking on the door of our consciousness. Unanswered, it is willing to take up habitation as a symptom, a disease, or a nightmare if it has to in order to not be ignored.

We are always creating the context within which we discover the meaning of life—our life. And even though we value the messages when they are direct, uncomplicated, cut and dried, most of our life is spent in a symbolic, emotional flux of insights, intuitions, metaphors, and mystery that when not understood by our ego is perfectly understood by our heart. When your heart "knows" that you are overlooking your true feelings, or that you are ignoring what you have already discovered is better for you, it will behave in ways that appear scary or symptomatic to get your attention. Unfortunately, when the heart speaks "its mind," physically or emotionally, with an additional accent of pounding, skipping, aching, or radiating sadness until we feel heavy hearted, we often panic and miss the deeper message. We then have a tendency to turn this heartful knowing into a symptom and fly to our mind seeking a remedy—a cure. When our mind and our heart are not in concert—when they become at odds with one another—we feel stressed, torn, ravaged, and we miss the deep knowing that is as close as a self-reflective conversation with our heart-centered wisdom.

While a dream speaks to you through metaphor, your heart will speak to you emotionally. You will feel the answer in a much more direct and less elusive manner if you have a trusting relationship to your feelings. Every memory whether awake or dreaming has an accompanying emotional component that makes sense to your heart.

Too often we disempower our self because of the potency of the emotion. Flooded with affect we drown in too much reactive meaning. Fear, not anger, is often the biggest culprit. Anger is a secondary feeling. By that I mean we use anger to cover up the primary feeling that, if revealed, would leave us even more vulnerable because it is in all likelihood more heart centered. You see, when you turn to your heart's wisdom about your true feelings they become more than reactions, they become embodied wisdom lessons. Check this out for yourself.

Discovering an Emotional Palette

We can never know ourselves completely until we allow ourselves to
be intimately connected to our heart-centered feelings. Otherwise
we will react *to* instead of interacting *with* our emotions. Anger is
probably one of the most familiar of our feelings because it engages
so much of our mind and body with its presence. However, anger is
always a secondary feeling preceded by another feeling that we are
too vulnerable to express.

- The next time you are angry, pause and see if you can name the
  feeling(s) that preceded the anger—embarrassment, sadness,
  loneliness, surprise, disappointment. . . . Trust your heart's wisdom
  to help you deepen into your vulnerability.

- Make a list of these deeper, less accessible feelings in your journal
  and add to it each time you notice a different one. For example:
  Are you angry—or caught off guard, feeling exposed, scared, agitated, impatient, irritated? These feelings may all be lumped
  together as anger, but each has its own select quality of information and emotion.

- Now take just one of these more vulnerable feelings and ask
  yourself what might have been going on instead of anger. Write
  your responses in your journal.

This exercise lends heart to your emotions. It is true that a picture can
be painted using only primary colors; however, the gradients and
subtleties will be left out. Think of this exercise as adding to your
emotional palette. Allow the different levels of feeling to add tone
and shade and texture to your emotional artistry. Review what you
have written as you get to know yourself better. Continue this exercise with each feeling until you have a heart-centered knowing about
the depth of your capacity for feeling. Remember, if you turn to your
heart and trust the knowing that is present there, you will never have

to sort out your feelings alone and confused. As you do this exercise, if you feel defensive, or full of explanations about why you feel as you do, remember the heart is nonjudgmental, non-defensive about what you are feeling. Stop, back up, and begin again, simply accepting who you are and what you felt and then move into exploring a deeper or different heart-centered feeling.

Fear Blurs the Message

Unlike anger, the emotion of fear is seldom secondary. Fear is more direct. It's true that fear can be learned—such as a fear of snakes—or it can be instinctual—for example, a fear of death—but the response is immediate and *always* visceral. Genuine fear gets you in your belly and your spine. *Unexamined,* any strong recurring emotion can define your life as surely as if you had a handicap or a deficit—bringing with it all sorts of other feelings about yourself and your ability to be fully in the world. Your heart may urge you to explore a possibility, but an unexamined fear will *automatically* freeze your desire and weaken your courage. In the grips of an unexamined emotion you are diminished—you become less than you are truly able to be. I'll tell you a dramatic story that illustrates this.

A friend of mine was extremely afraid of bugs of any sort. She had never really questioned her fear; all she remembered about its origins was that a cockroach had jumped on her, clinging to her arm when she was about three. Since then she had frozen if she crossed paths with any large or flying insect. She was positive that she could never cope with an environment that might expose her to a large insect.

One day as she was hemming a dress she noticed a strange black creature on the floor about two feet from her shoe. As she jumped up in alarm the creature jumped and landed almost at her feet. Horrified, her heart racing, she ran toward the stairs carrying her sewing with her. At the top of the stairs she turned and discovered to her increasing horror that this creature had followed her halfway up the stairs and so she fled, yelling for her husband. She dashed into the living room and jumped up on the sofa but the creature was close behind. Her husband arrived as she was crying and shaking and begging him to "kill it!" It turned out to be the partially unraveled thread from the hem of her dress. Black and all tangled up, it looked for the world to her eyes like a malevolent spider bent on getting her. I am certain if she had taken her own vital signs they would have registered the reality of her terror. Her body reacted to an image and past memories associated with the image as if what she believed she saw was an absolute reality. The thread looked like an insect, and my friend was propelled into the past—becoming three years old and terrified. If she had been able to confront her sense of utter vulnerability, consciously check out her perceptions, and realize that she could in fact protect herself as an adult, she would have been spared the agony of her fright. Looking back, my friend was able to see how many things she had avoided because of her unexamined fear that she was unable to take care of herself around insects. She was saddened by the way she had let her three-year-old's fear govern her life. Later she said she had never questioned her fear because she was so leery—so afraid—that even thinking about it would stir up all of her fear-filled reactions.

All too often, whether it's a symptom, a spontaneous reaction, a dream image that worries us, or an intuition that startles us, we avoid checking with our inner knowing for *fear* of where it may lead us. Avoidance is probably the single most strident foe of inner wisdom and self-esteem. Once your ego sounds the alarm, all body systems are flooded, and you are unlikely to turn to your heart, your intuition, or your soul for consultation. You cannot get to your inner knowing by way of avoidances. You will be refusing the very key or clue your soul is offering you that will lead to deeper understanding of your self. We all manage to gain insights as a result of trauma or chaos, but there is a better, more healthful way. Creating a center of calm receptivity within that you can turn to when you are gripped by not knowing is a far more heart-centered way.

There are many ways to practice calming yourself so that your first response after you feel fearful is to consult your heart. Then your sense of feeling ungrounded or confused (not knowing) can be transformed into insights as the deeper but obscured meaning of your experience is revealed. When you uncover the essential meaning, you will feel an instantaneous uplifting shift in your energy and your attitude.

In order to find the wisdom embedded in an emotion, you have to respect the presence of that emotion. By *respect* I mean that you must really take its presence and the accompanying affect to heart because there is an unclaimed vitality hidden within each emotion. You cannot find that vitality unless you are willing to consciously face whatever in you is tentative, fearful, or ambivalent about investing in your own strength and happiness. Fear blocks happiness. *Unexamined fear* blocks life.

HEART NOTES

Calming Yourself with Heart-Centered Knowing

You must be willing to take your emotions seriously—your heart certainly does, responding to every fluctuation of mood. Since we have been exploring fear in depth, we will focus on this emotion to demonstrate how you can allow the knowing of your heart to create a balanced calm when you are upset. Take your journal and go to your favorite quiet spot.

- Be aware of your most potent doubts or fears. At first limit your list to three choices. Speak them aloud and then write them down one at a time. When you write them down you can see them face to face, and they will take on more realistic proportions.

- Honor each doubt or fear by thinking about its effect upon your life and ask yourself if this is true now or if it is a remembered behavior (this may take several hours or even days). Write down what you discover. If it's an old and useless fear, pledge to let it go right now and reclaim the vitality it was blocking.

- Now place your list to one side and breathe deeply. Later, when you have learned more and are ready to release them, you may wish to write each item on its own piece of paper and burn it, or place them all in a box and bury them.

- Next, find a happy memory—one that fills you with warm and relaxed feelings. Take your time and revisit every detail of this recollection. If you can't recall a particularly happy memory, go to a time when you ate something you completely enjoyed, or when you saw something that you really liked looking at. Hold this memory in your imagination and place it within your heart. Breathe into the memory, allowing the positive feeling to fill your mind and body. Allow yourself to be fully conscious of the feeling of being infused with happiness. *This happiness is real.* It is yours, and no one and nothing can take it away from you.

- Now, imagine the chambers of your heart as a beautiful sanctuary, always waiting to receive you. One at a time, take each fear from your list and place it in your heart, and ask your heart where the hidden vitality is. What does your heart know that you do not know? Write the answer down. Then move to the next fear on your list and repeat this process until you have done so with every item on your list.

Practice this on a regular basis until it becomes second nature. You can use this exercise anytime you are stressed or fearful. Go to the positive memory first—allow it to fill your heart and radiate into your body and calm your mind. Then imagine yourself placing the stress or fear in the chamber of your heart to be cleansed, relieved of its potency. Ask your heart's energy how to respond to your feelings. Almost immediately you'll find you feel much more in charge of your life.

Reading the Signals

As you already know, when I speak of the *bodymind* I am referring to the energy intelligence of your cellular body. When I speak of the *bodysoul* I am speaking of the essential self—the embodied soul that is the essence of your human beingness. You cannot claim to be fully in charge of yourself until you develop familiarity and trust in the less familiar languages of your bodymind as it responds to the desires of your embodied soul. Without a trusting familiarity with your feelings, your ego will read every disturbance as troublesome and mobilize the "guards" to eradicate some of your most vital experiences.

Every moment of your life, waking or sleeping, is filled with the symbolic images, the untapped emotions, and the physical sensations of your *unlived* life: your yearning, your unplumbed potential, your deepest desires. You are not a dumb mechanical body that is governed and animated by an intellect that is housed in your brain. You are an exquisitely spiritual being that is learning to fully express the depth and breadth of your embodied knowing while inhabiting a human form. This means that mind and body and soul are seamless. Every cell of your matter has a wisdom and an intelligence of its own that is both innately physical and incarnately spiritual. That intelligence has many, many ways to express its presence. It may speak to you through a symptom, a persistent memory, a symbol, a dream, a hunger, or even existential grief—the deep yearning for something unfathomable, just outside of your consciousness.

Heartfelt Validation

Recently, while wondering if I was on the right path with the manuscript for this book, I received an unexpected gift of a blank book with hearts all over the cover. I smiled and thought, *What a lovely coincidence.* Immediately my heart skipped a beat. *What? What am I overlooking?* I wondered. Later in the day a client came in and wanted to talk about a biblical story concerning *doubt and losing sight of the intended path*. When the hour was over I realized that my casual dismissal of Spirit's symbolic message on the cover of the book as *merely a coincidence* troubled my heart. Yet, as if the greater intelligence of the universe wished for my attention, my client brought me the same message in a slightly different way. After all, if I haven't the heart for recognizing validation and encouragement, then how real can I possibly be as I follow my *intended path* and write a book about the heart's wisdom? It's so easy to forget that proof is the mind's way. Validation is the way of the heart. Validation takes root in a casual remark, an unexpected gift, a telephone message, or a dream image. Validation moves steadily and softly, taking up habitation in your bones and cells and soul. Your ego may seek concrete direction—your heart resonates with validation.

In a town not far from where I live, there is a woman who is convinced that she has an annual visitation from the Virgin Mary. Each anniversary thousands of people come to her farm for a few hours for healing, to pray, and to listen. One visitor echoed what most were feeling after the news reported skepticism about this woman's sanity, her credibility, and her intentions. One visitor said, "I don't have to have proof of her credibility, my heart tells me something deeply moving is happening here and that alone is reason enough for me to believe that I am better for having come. In today's busy world it is rare to find anything that moves my heart."

What seems to trouble the scientifically oriented most is lack of proof. How can one measure, quantify, and replicate this knowing of the heart to ensure that it is the "real stuff," worth listening to and following instead of a fantasy or worse—hysteria? How can we be certain that this so-called cellular intelligence is not just an artifact of excitation, or that we are not reading too much into the ordinary innate hormonal and muscular functions of the physical body?

Ever since Dr. W. Penfield, the nineteenth-century surgeon, inserted a probe into the human brain and his patient was able to recall in detail sights, sounds, and even conversations associated with long-forgotten memories, these questions have tantalized and troubled modern humankind. Dr. Candace Pert's benchmark research, published in 1997, in uncovering the amino acid chains that allow the researcher to track the cellular intelligence of the emotional body has certainly thrown scientific skepticism into disarray. The once entrenched medical position about psychosomatic illness being "all in the patient's head" has been reevaluated, as medicine and research have created an entire field of mindbody medicine. As Pert so aptly puts it, "If you have a gut feeling listen, your gut knows something you need to know."

Is it possible that there is evidence of the incarnate, embodied soul? Could we possibly be in touch with what Dr. Paul Pearsall, author and psychoneuroimmunologist, calls the "soul's code" as it is conveyed by our heart? Everything we have learned so far leads us to believe that the old rules and guidelines aren't enough to help us answer this question. It appears that we have to be willing to set aside our trusted microscopes, our stethoscopes, even our weights and measures, and open our minds and our hearts to the growing number of contemporary storytellers, like Claire in chapter 3, as they tell us of their experiences with the heart and its immense soulful "knowing."

Healing the Split

Today there are many stories about nonverbal wisdom, about cellular memory and the unplumbed electromagnetic "language" of the heart. We have had to replace our mind/body split with a recognition that we live with the dual intelligences of the mind and the heart constantly informing one another, which in turn informs us. Historically, due to the mind–over–matter posture, we have also been taught that rationale, the "logic" of the brain, is superior to the symbolic, emotional, and hence, illogic, of our heart. This view is a matter of custom and experience, not embodied evidence. Drs. Pearsall, Gary Schwartz, Linda Russek, Pert, and a whole host of others are showing us that although our brain does lend us the capacity for spoken language, the heart is equally articulate using the language of symptoms and embodied intuition. This language brings to consciousness the thoughts and the feelings that make just as much sense in your life as the more structured syntax of spoken words. Your brain thinks, ordering the disparate pieces of emotion and associations into a gestalt, a more complete picture, so that image forms instantaneous meaning. Your heart is more gifted with feeling, and each, thinking and feeling, is equally intelligent, speaking to you moment by moment. Your brain is far more adaptive to external influences, making it socially oriented. Your heart is fiercely personal, intimately invested in you and your embodied energies. If you wish to learn to care soulfully for yourself, you will want to note that *your brain strives for dominance while your heart seeks unity.* Your brain is relentlessly evaluative while your heart is deeply relational. The electromagnetic field, the pulsing, radiant life force of your heart is 5,000 times stronger than that of your brain. *Long before your brain has sorted something out your heart simply knows.* In fact the cardio-energy researchers now believe that our brain does not orchestrate our lives—the heart does, and the brain follows the heart's lead. This may be why we can reason ourselves out of something only to have our emotions or a symptom indicate that we are on the wrong track.

It's true that we can't always live by the heart's reasoning. Sometimes life circumstances require very difficult heart-rending decisions—decisions and choices that "break" something carried by your heart. Maybe it's love or commitment or purpose and you know that even though the cost causes your heart to ache, circumstances require you to do it. Still, to harden your heart in order to go against your soul's purpose is more costly than allowing your heart to break with conscious awareness. Unless you are willing to allow your heart to break open with the sorrows of life, it cannot expand and grow large enough to embrace all that you are capable of loving. Nor will you be able to be open enough to accept all the love that you are offered.

What Do You Believe About Your Soul?

As you sit here reading I ask you, Do you believe you are vitalized by a soul? Where would you locate it? Take a moment and place your hand there, please. Now I want you to ask yourself, "What would it mean to believe, *really believe,* that my heart carries a cellular imprint, a knowing of my deepest yearnings, that it is a repository for what is vitally important to my spiritual growth, and it carries this knowing for a period of time even if it is beating in the chest of another?" *Isn't this possibility worth exploring in order to check it out with your own experiences?*

Stop for a minute and let's review some other mysterious but more familiar knowledge that is contained by your bodysoul. You know about phantom limb syndrome, where after the loss of a limb there remain such strong sensations that there is an undeniable urge to scratch the missing leg or toes or fingers. Amputated, the body memories remain, the nerve endings won't just forget. Out of sight, out of mind won't work here. And there is the real physical mystery of multiple personality disorder. In this disorder a single individual will exhibit several different personalities, each with its own set of physical symptoms, body postures, memories, and other distinguishing traits. One personality may be dominant right and the other dominant left. One may have a severe allergy to a substance that the other shows absolutely no reaction to. Another personality may be severely nearsighted but when she switches to a different personality she can see perfectly well.

Or, there's the arresting phenomenon of meeting someone we've never met before and feeling that we know them very well. Our brain may tell us this is absurd, but our heart tells us we have met a "soul sister or brother." I once had this happen to me with a grasshopper! I was sitting on a bench in a park waiting for my children to finish playing when a large green and red grasshopper jumped onto the walkway about ten feet away. Immediately I felt his attention directed my way, and I had the unsettling feeling that he wanted to come over to me. I sat quietly talking to him as bit by bit he approached. Finally he hopped to a foot or so away and stared in my direction. Time stood still, and I had the distinct impression that we two were meant to be right here, right now. I inclined my head in respectful recognition, and he turned rapidly and in one gigantic, thrusting leap was gone. I can't speak for brother grasshopper, but I felt moved, softened, touched. My head was only mildly interested, but my heart felt nourished by this very special and particular encounter. There are so many incidences that extend beyond what can be logically or rationally explained but that affect us deeply nonetheless. The respectful attention we give them helps to define who we are and what we believe about life's value. The enemy of living fully connected to Nature through your nature is *the fear of being judged by others. Don't wait until you are dying to discover that those others reside mostly in your own imagination.*

HEART NOTES

Trusting in Your Heart's Intention

Can you allow yourself to trust that pausing and sincerely listening to your heart's version of truth can nurture and nourish you in every possible way? I believe you will find that this simple practice of trust done five minutes every day can sustain you.

- Think about what you really believe about your relationship to your soul.

- Now ask yourself, "What do I harbor about myself within my heart, either not daring to bring it into reality or waiting for a later time, a better opportunity? If my heart was beating in the chest of another, what would it carry of my essence within it?"

- Write down your thoughts and insights in your journal so that you can continue to review them when you want to.

- Now write a letter to yourself telling your head what your heart knows. Tell your head how these insights will change the way you think and feel about yourself.

- Promise yourself that each time you return to an old pattern of thought that neglects these heart truths, you will turn to your heart and get recentered—recommitted.

In learning to love yourself as much as your heart already loves you it is important to live your life consciously and with intentional love for everything in your life that seems to defeat you.

Opening the door to your heart opens the door to your passions, allowing you to own them and express them. Trusting your heart to lead you, you no longer waste precious vitality protecting yourself in the old, inhibited ways. Passion—a hunger to live fully—is the heart's joy.

CHAPTER 5

What Your Heart Wants

Deep listening from the heart is one half
of true communication.
Speaking from the heart is the other half.

—SARA PADDISON

On the first night of gathering at many of the retreats I lead I place a "talking stick" on the altar that has been created on the floor in the middle of our circle of chairs. This talking stick is an object—sometimes a carved stick, and at other times a handheld microphone—that has been tied with red streamers and a branch of sage. I have adapted both the talking stick and its use from a Native American practice. The intention of this practice is to remind each person as he or she picks up the stick that what is said should be brief and *only the truth*—that the words should come from the heart and represent essence. Then each participant, in turn, by picking up the stick as he speaks his name agrees to the conditions of this invitation. From our very first meeting we are pledged to speak from what our heart knows and wants to express, not what our head wants others to believe. Each speaker quickly learns an even deeper truth: You cannot speak from your heart unless you are willing to listen to your heart. Your heart knows what your soul wants.

Listening to Your Heart's Wanting

Best friends and running buddies Marianne and Sharon ran nearly every day. When the Avon Run for Breast Cancer sent out the invitation for women to run for their cause, the two women didn't miss a beat. They were among the first to sign up. All was going well with their training walks until Marianne began to lose interest. Surprised and disappointed, she confided to Sharon that she "had lost her heart for this effort." Sharon, more than a little curious, asked her when her loss of heart had begun. The answer, hard to pinpoint at first, emerged as the two women continued to talk until Marianne remembered a passing thought that deeply affected her interest.

She was leaving the theater after seeing a boring movie when she began to have the nagging thought that she had been wasting a lot of her adult life on empty activities. Deeper probing led her to realize she was doing many things that really held no energy or attraction for her at all. *When,* she wondered, *did I begin to settle for boredom as a way of life? When did I decide that resignation to boredom is my only option?* For the first time in a long time, Marianne was asking herself serious questions about her life. She was waking up to the realities versus the illusions. She was beginning to suspect she had been living much of her life as if she were sleepwalking.

Alone later, as these thoughts continued, she found herself becoming increasingly aware of the way she really felt about how she was living her life. *When,* she thought, *was I ever truly real about who and what I want for myself? When did I last take myself seriously enough to say No to the empty pursuits? And why on Earth not?*

Her job, she told Sharon that sunny morning as they sat on the grass and talked, was a bore. "I am successful, if salary is any measure. Here I sit with a promising future in advertising and I really don't like what I'm doing or how much time I have to spend doing it. My heart isn't in that either. I get up in the morning and need a new outfit or an exciting bit of gossip to get me inspired enough to go into the office. It's never the creative challenge I thought it would be when I was a kid dreaming of a city career. Last night I asked myself if I had the courage to chuck it all, and even that didn't excite me."

Sharon, fearing her friend was depressed and without a solution to her lethargy, tried at first to bolster her morale, and then realized that Marianne was echoing something she too had given attention to, but only at night when she couldn't sleep—or in the early morning before her day had begun. For Sharon it was where and how she was living. Long an active member of two professional organizations, a church group, and several other social groups, she rushed between meetings and deadlines in order to squeeze in beloved exercise time at her local Y and bemoaned ever having enough time for herself. She had waited years to move to the city and now found herself drawn into traffic gridlock and escalating crowds each time she left her home. Her life was not what she had imagined it would become. Startled by this insight, she asked herself, *When and how did I lose that vision, those dreams?*

Sharpening Your Senses

It takes a lot of energy to dull our senses so that we no longer listen to our soul's voice, we no longer turn to our heart. As we approach adulthood we can hardly wait to be on our own. We are eager to move out into the world and leave behind the familiar roles and identities that we have carried since childhood. For the first time, we tell ourself, for the *first time I'll really be me*. What no one tells us is that moving, finding a job, getting married, starting a career is only the first step in being authentic—in developing a heart-honest relationship with ourself.

In the excitement or the discouragement and hard work that engulf us, we become distracted, detached from our dreams and our desires to be who or what we've always anticipated we can be. Detachment is the way the frightened ego attempts to avoid what it cannot understand or control. Mahatma Gandhi said it well when he said that our greatness lies not so much in being able to change the world as it does in being able to change ourselves. To authentically change one's self requires involvement with your essence—your heart's desires. This relationship propels us into an awareness of the deeply intrapersonal realm of our being and its intimate relationship to the transpersonal realm of Spirit or God.

You cannot stay detached from the truly important questions about your life once you turn to the affects of your embodied soul. Then the experience goes beyond thought or speculation—your heart is touched and you can feel its responsiveness right in your body. Or, your God Spot is awakened. Your God Spot, a term coined by researchers, is a cluster of neurons within the temporal lobes of your brain that responds immediately and systemically whenever you feel connected to something deeply meaningful, flooding your body with an uplifting sense of peace and love. Life matters, and we carry its evidence in the very matter that forms our body and houses our soul. *When we ignore what matters most to us, then it will become the matter with us.* Symptoms inevitably follow.

Next comes the hardest part. Consciousness. A life lived honestly and with truth will reveal all the little dishonesties, all the illusions and pettiness we hang onto to excuse our sleepwalking. A life lived honestly and authentically is hard work. When you make listening to what your heart wants a priority, your life shifts, and you begin to be present to your capacity to stay centered and undisturbed by the ups and downs of life. Internally you develop an unshakable sense of guidance—of presence.

Founder of the HeartMath Institute Doc Childre, in his book written with Bruce Cryer, *From Chaos to Coherence,* underscores the deep and sustaining value of presence. He poses the question, "Could presence be heart-generated coherence in the world of personal magnetics? People with presence," he continues, "have an ineffable quality about them; they are 'present,' surprisingly attentive and undistracted. A fullness, a centeredness, a wholeness radiates from them."

Presence can be cultivated as you begin the process of reviewing the chaos in your life—reviewing those things that create discordance. At first we are shocked to realize that the love relationship or marriage or even the housemate that was supposed to help us feel independent and special has somehow become a replication of the very thing we wished to escape. We feel just as insecure, misunderstood, or uncertain as we did before we set out on our own. And no surprise. When we make our relationship choice unconsciously we are always immediately drawn to the one that is most familiar—that carries the dynamics we have been trying to escape. Unconscious, we have no choice but to gravitate in the direction of the familiar even when we've sworn to ourselves we won't. Unconsciousness guarantees repetition. Unconscious repetition numbs the soul and dulls the heart, while completely bypassing the wisdom of the deep self. We succumb to boredom and don't inhabit our body or consult our bodymind. Sometimes depression is another way of describing the absence of any meaningful relationship to a higher calling, a purpose for being. Without this, we find we have little or no personal conviction. And yet if we risk questioning the dull or the deadening or the dream that keeps nagging at us, we have begun to move toward an understanding of what the heart wants us to learn by questioning what the ego would have us settle for. Bit by bit, presence follows.

Nowhere in our schooling or our dinner table conversations did anyone tell us to be prepared for the inevitability of a conflict between our mind and our heart. If they had, they might have begun by telling us that our ego and its marvelous capacity to learn, to reason, and to negotiate would only take us so far. They would have been quick to point out that the ego is adaptive, a very highly functioning coping mechanism. A strong ego is of immeasurable value, but it certainly is not all that we are. We would have been told that the day would come when we would feel the need to make meaning out of our world, and reason and logic alone would not be enough. And further they would say, when that day arrives you will finally hear, really hear the poet Rumi's words when he writes, "Look for someone else to tend the shop. I'm out of the image making business" as an invitation to you personally. Someone might have prepared us to expect that the day would come when we would stop dead in our tracks and ask ourself, "What, if anything, is my life all about?"

The "Instinct of Truth"

An instinct isn't learned, it's visceral. There is an instinct for deep personal truth that resides within each of us. Its truth is unshakable and sternly requiring. Instinctual truth can't be unearthed by thinking alone; it begs for a soulful emotional inventory and for sincere and courageous self-examination. We brush up against it and it frightens us with its intensity. *Speak up,* the heart urges, but the timid little ego says, *Settle for what is easier, what is available. Who do you think you are anyhow? Who do you know that ever got anywhere by following their heart? Sentimental bilge!!!* Yet one day, if we are lucky, we realize that the voice we thought was outside of us is really inside of us. We have been handing our heart's vision over to a bogus tyrant—an internal Wizard of Oz, all threats and admonishments but no substance at all. The terms of battle are clear. The ego says, *Make the choice to claim your own life and you* may *die.* The heart says, *Don't make the choice to claim your own life and you* will *die.* You will die the slow death of knowing in your heart of hearts that you never truly risked being authentic—choosing to live from your particular and unique instinct of truth.

There may be physical evidence of an embodied instinct for truth. Drs. Danah Zohar and Ian Marshall in their book, *SQ: Connecting with Our Spiritual Intelligence,* present a valid and moving description of the God Spot. The authors make the argument that when this spot is stimulated, as it is spontaneously in temporal lobe epilepsy, the individual has visions of the transcendent, of great beauty and a sense of spiritual certitude. By this I don't mean religious certitude, but rather the belief that there is a profound sense of meaning to life, a sense of purpose. Scientists have designed a helmet lined with sensors that can both measure the temporal lobe activity of the entire skull and record the results on a graph. They found that those persons who wore it while describing a deeply meaningful experience or a personal relationship to beauty or something transcendent all had a response from the same cluster of temporal lobe nerve cells—their God Spot. These cells lit up and sent out a rhythmic wave of energy from the front of the skull to the back. This wave was coherent, soothing, uniting. There is, according to these accounts, a core energy that resides within our cellular structure that when activated allows us to feel our connection to a larger picture, a vaster source of meaning. We humans call this by many names—I am calling it *soul.*

In their book, Zohar and Marshall list the eight revitalizing qualities present in a spiritually intelligent person:

1. Flexibility

2. Self-awareness

3. Idealism (a capacity to be vision- and value-led)

4. A capacity to use suffering transformatively

5. An openness to diversity (welcoming inquiry into anything or anyone that shakes up the system)

6. A genuine desire to ask, *Why?*

7. An ability to see the bigger picture, and

8. A tolerance for spontaneity.

In other words, the adult ability to have a child's open and inquiring mind. It would appear that when any one of these qualities is strongly activated, the emotional response starts the desire for connection to a more Spirit-filled life.

When you feel this energy throughout your body you don't need explanations, you are being fed by the experience. Just as a plant turns toward the streaming sunlight, your body pulses with the streaming energy that cascades from the God Spot. Just as a green shoot droops and withers without sunlight, so your body and soul retreat and lose luster and vitality without the radiance created by the image or memory of transpersonal love. Some of us shudder to call anything "God" since we have been so damaged by a male-centered, organized religion. I urge you not to allow a name to daunt you. Please call it your Deep Feminine Spot, or Universal Spirit Spot—you choose—the reality is in the response not the social connotations.

Fortunately we don't have to learn to rely upon our ego to connect us to this energy. In fact, you probably can't rely upon your ego alone, since the ego resists metaphysical realities for fear of the loss of its own power and turns the accompanying physical responses into symptoms to be cured, not appreciated. An image, an illness, a loss, a moment of beauty, countless moments can and do stir us into the awareness of our yearning to consciously embody our relationship to our God/Goddess Spot. Our dreams, our symptoms, and our sixth and seventh senses urge us to discover who we truly are and what we must believe in order to be true to our core self. The strong relationship between your heart and your brain unite to ensure that you are on the right track. No amount of searching and listening can replace a trusting relationship with your heart's wisdom.

A Wider Picture

Now we return to Sharon and Marianne, who have risked a brief look at the meaning of their lives; their openness about their quest is about to capture the interest of others.

By agreement, for the next two days each woman independently shared her dilemma with a total of eleven friends, leading Sharon and Marianne to discover that they were anything but alone in their discouragement. Like an electrical jolt, their stories infused their friends with a desire to soul search. One after another, all eleven indicated a willingness to do some serious reevaluation of their lives. They agreed that this reevaluation had to include complete honesty about their emotions—how they felt about what they discovered.

The instinct of truth is always heart connected. Because it is on the side of life, it attracts others who are ready to face their own ambivalence about authenticity. Because it is on the side of life, it offers the possibility of creativity and spontaneity. Because it is on the side of life, it offers vitality.

Sharon and Marianne agreed that they felt compelled to take a long hard look at how their desire for approval or social success was governing their lives. To make your choices by constantly seeking approval, as Rachel Naomi Remen says so exquisitely, "is to have no resting place, no sanctuary.... It makes us uncertain of who we are and of our true value."

It seems that out of the group of eleven male and female friends, only two—one man and one woman—were truly satisfied with their life choices. The man, a landscaper, said he'd known

> since I was a kid that I wanted to garden, to be outside and create beautiful naturescapes. I have pursued this love even though by many standards I'm thought of as an underachiever when it comes to fast bucks and owning lots of material goods. I tried other careers but nothing gave me any joy. I even completed a degree in engineering. Since I was heir apparent to my mother's

engineering firm it seemed crazy to give up a guaranteed future. It didn't take me long to realize I could do my job well, even enjoy it at times, but I didn't have a single day when I woke up eager to go to the office. Now I have to tell you I lost a fiancée because of my return to landscaping. She felt I was untrustworthy by saying No to engineering and Yes to dirt. Sometimes there is heartache in following your heart's desire.

The woman Leila, one of a set of twins whose sister died when they were eleven, said she never wanted to be anything but a dancer with her twin, so she went into mime and created a balletic mime show that she and her partner have been in for over ten years. They plan, choreograph, and perform as a team. She remarked,

> I'm under no illusion that Shirley [her partner] is a substitute for my dead twin. After her death I felt a loss so profound that to this day I can't do it justice with words alone. It was an amputation. My heart and soul were severed in two, and her half was forever beyond my reach. I prayed and prayed for a way to feel her presence and my twinnedness. I wanted to be shown how to dance for both of us. Gradually I began to recognize that there was something more. I had to find a way to honor our relationship and also be true to myself. I've always known I was meant to dance this way, intimately and happily partnered. You may think it's a dramatic exaggeration, but I've felt this calling to me since I was too young to really have anything but a vision, an image, a dream of the future and what was waiting for me. Not fame, but fulfillment, sacred fulfillment, like a prayer that gets lived out.

"Heartbreak was exactly what convinced me to follow my heart." This remark by Leila, the surviving twin, was met with nods of recognition.

> God knows when my sister died I felt more than lost—she was the other half of my soul-self! I used to go walking and pretend

my shadow was really her walking several steps behind me. But walking and pretense are poor substitutes for dancing and I knew deep in my soul that dancing was—is—a life's purpose for me. So I kept that ache alive to remind me that I HAD to dance, and with a partner.

I can't begin to tell you how much I believed in my bones that dancing is what I am destined to do. When I tuned into my heart-soul I felt like singing each time I imagined a partner who wordlessly, intuitively both led and followed my lead. When I imagined dancing alone the joy left. So I began dancing in response to my own reflections in the full-length studio mirrors. One day I instinctually began miming myself. As my heart began to race I felt alive, more alive than since K.'s death. It was then I knew that I had been led to the one way we could continue our destiny as twins. I carry her in my heart, and I know even after I am too old to dance I will feel fulfilled and at peace.

Journey into Wholeness

For more than twenty years I have lectured and led seminars for an organization called Journey into Wholeness. This organization, which blends the psychology of Swiss psychiatrist Carl Jung and the principles of Christianity, began as a heartfelt calling for its founder, Annette Cullipher. There is a beautiful prayer that is spoken at every Journey into Wholeness Conference. Written by George Appleton, it echoes Sharon and Marianne's awakening.

> Give me a candle of the Spirit, Oh God,
> as I go down into the deep of my own being.
> Show me the hidden things.
> Take me down to the spring of my life,
> and tell me my nature and my name.
> Give me the freedom to grow so that I may become

my true self—the fulfillment of the seed that you planted
in me at my making. . . .

The sorrow of modern humankind is that we yearn to find a way to
marry the sacred with the secular. Another way to say this is that we
long to bring the sacred into our ordinary, everyday existence in a
meaningful way. When we know what our core nature and our
embodied name is, then most of what we do, no matter how boring,
can be done from the true self, with heart. When we are able to
touch into that deeply rooted sense of what is right for this life and
our part in it, we touch into our embodied instinct of truth. Life
takes on meaning and purpose. Bit by bit we begin to love the person
that we have become. Carl Jung's life work, his life's purpose, was to
urge those who had the courage for it to grow into their fullest personhood—to find and serve one's spiritual calling while continuing
to be a baker, a homemaker, a poet. Jung felt from his own life's experiences that one must never cease seeking whatever allows one to
feel true to something greater than oneself.

This calling doesn't necessarily bring fame and wealth and power.
Nor does it protect one from pain, suffering, or disappointments.
Instead it brings a peace of mind, a strength of soul, and a sense of
enduring purpose rooted in that *seed that was planted in you at your conception—your spiritual incarnation*. This seed carries the promise of
your unfolding life's purpose—your heart's desire.

HEART NOTES

Recalling Yourself

The stirrings of destiny begin very early in life. Usually with the first
shock of individuality. Do you remember the very first time you
became conscious of yourself as a separate being? What was the
experience like? Take the time to find a picture of yourself as an infant

or a young child. Place it, along with your journal and your mirror, next to your chair.

- Place the picture where you can see it, and then in your journal write down every detail you remember about the first time you became conscious of yourself as an individual. This usually happens around age three, although I've heard stories from as early as age two.
- Write down this little one's experience as you remember it.
- Now take your mirror and look into your eyes. See the eyes of that first experience gazing back at you, and be appreciative for this child's journey.
- Remember how you felt about yourself then, and write down how that experience has influenced who you are today.

You may want to create your own ceremony of remembrance and your coming of age now that you are more fully conscious of your uniqueness in this body and this lifetime. Maybe a simple declaration, such as, *This is who I am—at my deepest and most private core. I need no one to validate me—I am my own authentic self. Divinely centered and rooted in this earth, this matter.*

This remembrance is the beginning of claiming intimacy with your true self, your core identity. It is said that in early childhood we still stand close to our remembrance of our relationship with Spirit before our birth, allowing us to have memorable imaginary experiences with this core knowing. There is a deeply held sense of wanting to be called, of wanting to discover and follow a deeper and more meaningful path. One day we just *know* that it is time to wake up to the soul-searching and find out just exactly who lives within us.

Children Know What Their Hearts Want

Adults don't seem to realize that children often have deep life-directing inner experiences that they keep to themselves. Open to the vastness of life and the seamlessness between the galaxy of their interior world and life, children have imaginary friends, dolls, or animals that guide and support them and angels, fairies, and all manner of spirits that are very real, very important teachers.

The conversations and fantasies shared with these companions come from a depth of imagination that exceeds what a three-year-old is supposed to know. Since the child is both author and actor in these "imaginary" dramas, the wisdom may be childlike, but it is anything but childish. It springs from an inner source—an attentive inner guidance that only the child can tap into.

Trusting, we, like children, often turn to our imaginations for comfort, for reassurance, and to answer the questions that touch our hearts. These experiences are soul experiences—the connections are felt in our hearts, not our heads. The words or images that come to us at these times are messages from our deeper self—our soulful heart. Usually these experiences fade away, but some incidents occur in childhood that our soul is presenting to show us the path to our destiny, to the seed that was planted in us at our conception, if we listen.

I often smile when I remember my favorite childhood game. I loved to collect small memo pads and cast-off pencils, which I kept in a cigar box. Every time I got to go to the local novelty store with my grandfather I'd ask for "supplies." Then at home I'd take a card table and extend only two legs. Sitting in an overstuffed living room chair I'd pull the table toward me and rest it on the arms of the chair, making a makeshift desk. There I'd play happily for hours with my "writing." Today I am most heart-centered when I am writing.

Looking back, you can probably discern a thread of connection begun in childhood that seems to be leading you, pulling some may say, toward your destiny. The knowing of your heart often first presents itself to the child as a beloved pastime or a favorite reverie or a well-loved fairy tale character. Little did I know at age three and four, especially since I don't come from a college-educated family, that someday my "papers" would lead to a doctorate and the publication of two books. Accepting responsibility for finding and following this thread can be a lifelong quest. You cannot recognize it if you refuse to believe it is there. One of the more graphic ways to do this is to list all the times you've really wanted something or have been close to reaching your goal when the door has been slammed shut. Instead of collecting your "losses" as evidence of life's unfairness, see if you can discover how those slammed doors redirected you—maybe you were knocking on the wrong door anyway.

HEART NOTES

Collecting Your Losses

Take time to do this as an exercise in recognizing how your soul has stopped you from making a choice that would have led you away from what your heart wants. You'll need your journal.

- List your major disappointments in life.
- Now look at them as redirections that prevented you from making an incorrect choice.
- See if you can find a pattern or a thread of guidance that you never noticed before. Describe this pattern in detail in your journal.
- How is your life better because of these disappointments? Write this down.
- Examine each disappointment as guidance from your heart. Where did each one eventually lead you? Record each insight so you can reread and marvel at the pattern. How might you be more authentic by consciously being appreciative?
- Create a ritual to thank your heart for wanting you to follow your soul's purpose by writing each disappointment on a different piece of colored paper and burning them in a container on your

altar or outside in a quiet private ceremony. Scatter the ashes in nature.

Your heart knows what is wanting—what is lacking—in your life far better than you do. Listen and follow its lead.

Destiny or Fate

Carl Jung has the best description that I know of about how soul's presence or lack plays out during each lifetime. He says that we each have the choice to live our lives consciously or unconsciously. Consciousness to Jung means listening to the soul and learning how to live life authentically, with heart. This, he says, will inevitably lead us to our destiny, where we feel centered and connected to our own essence. Here life has meaning and purpose no matter how mundane our pursuits appear to others. That fine Persian poet Rumi once penned these lines about life and death—about consciousness and unconsciousness:

> We may worry about death, but what worries the soul
>   the most
> is to have never fully tasted the waters of its own essence.

For you never to have lived your life in an essential way, never knowing that your choices came from a deeply embodied conscious sense of what is right for you and you alone at this time, leaves you in the hands of fate.

Fate, says Jung, is a life lived unconsciously, our choices made as if we have no choice or for reasons that exclude what our heart wants us to consider. Here life feels tedious and empty. We develop an aversion to questioning our own motives or looking carefully at where our decisions may lead. What is not brought to consciousness has no choice but to be lived out as fate. The unlived life is loss enough, but the *unexamined* life is a terrible unnecessary loss.

Handing one's life over to fate is spiritually self-destructive. You may not believe it at first, then one day you realize that your creative energies have fled and you have cut off the fragile threads of your own hopes. Wishing for life to happen is never the same as actively making your life happen. And there are discomforts, since conscious choice stirs up all sorts of tension. There will always be conflict between the easier road to fateful acceptance of "our lot in life" and the tougher road to authenticity. Until you wake up to the reality that the soul is not afraid of conflict, not when the stakes are your embodied instinct for truth, you may incorrectly blame life instead of your own unconsciousness for letting you down. Your heart is a sounding board, a compass, a companion who knows you better than you often know yourself and will not let you down. Your heart carries within it the designs for your destiny. Destiny introduces the catalyst of personhood, of choosing—of individuation.

When Marianne and Sharon's friends said they had "known" since childhood what would enrich their lives they were undoubtedly describing a nonverbal sense of just knowing, a sense of heartfelt inner security and peace. No words or direct guidance appeared, yet they "knew" nonetheless. They felt its affirming vitality. The man and woman among this friendship group who had managed to hold onto this knowing were committed to making the choices and *sacrifices* that guided them closer to their heart's desire—their soul's essence. *Knowing* is a deeply felt sense of correctness, unspoken but resonantly influential nonetheless. No words are needed; the feelings are enough.

We each can learn to recognize what we desire as easily as Sharon and Marianne recognized what they didn't. The hardest step is believing that there is indeed a cellular spiritual intelligence that always knows what is best for you even when your head doesn't. Your heart is a magnificent tuning fork in this regard. Your heart's vibrations "speak" volumes on your soul's behalf. Your relationship with your soul can't be sorted out by your head—it has to be a way of life, of being—a sincere honoring of incarnation. And for this reason alone you will not wish to turn your desire to know what your heart wants you to know over to chance.

If I Were the King of the World

It's a familiar child's game. If I were the king if the world—or the universe—I would be. . . . If my parents had loved me more or I had a good relationship, or enough money or my health. . . . If I were only in charge of my own destiny. . . .

Each of us must find something—the courage or the despair or the curiosity that will keep us drawn to the task of uncovering heart-centered authenticity. No one can do this for anyone else. Not an astrologer or a therapist or a great book. These things may help, but ultimately no one can do this for you but yourself. Transformation begins after the first *committed* step of this journey. Because when you make a commitment you are also opening your heart to all the parts of yourself that you have rejected or ignored. Then the neglected comes forward to greet you, and without a commitment the task is just too great—too overwhelming. We are not talking about a monumental occurrence, but rather an undeniable awakening to how much of your day-to-day existence begs to be more purposeful—*more consciously engaged by you.*

Anne, sharing a page from her journal, reminds us how this can and does happen during the most ordinary of activities.

> I have saved up time off and today I begin a delicious four days to review my life and take an inventory. First I think I'll do the breakfast dishes so I won't have a messy kitchen. As I am wiping down the table I notice these flowers really need fresh water and it will only take a second. Whoops, several are quite ratty, dead and not at all attractive. Well no problem I can just take them out

and clean up the counter after I throw them away. Finally I start toward my chair, my journal—favorite pen in hand—when I remember I wanted to run some mail down to the curbside mailbox so it will go out today. As I reenter the house I glance at the clock and feel a familiar sinking feeling—two hours—where did the time go? Maybe I'll get an early start immediately after lunch since most of this morning is gone anyhow. As I am preparing lunch I feel the gloom descend. Another morning—a precious time-apart morning—has slipped through my hands. This morning was to be a pledge to begin to live my life more consciously and without even protesting I have gone brain-dead and let it just slip away. So much of my life has evaporated just this way—so unnoticed that there has been no one to mourn its passing. I feel heartsick.

A commitment to look within and ask what your heart wants stirs up the debris of unlived promise, of the dreams and hopes and desires and loves that wait naked, disowned, and pulsing beneath our rib cage—sheltered by our heart. Far too often life intervenes and we put off the quest until after lunch. Your heart carries the magnetic energy that is radiant with your soul's purpose—with your core essence—your root identity—waiting, just waiting for you to turn your attention in its direction.

Root Identity

Muriel sent me this quote from author Emily Hancock. "At the buried core of a woman's identity is a distinct and vital self first articulated in childhood, a root identity that gets cut off in the process of growing up. . . ." Emily is speaking especially about females since this is the focus of her work, but this is true for every one of us—men as well as women. Part of the pain we suffer is the mistaken notion that men don't have the same needs and feelings that women do. If I removed the gender references and names from the stories included in this book we would not be able to tell the gender of the writer. The soul is not gender prejudiced—the heart beats no gender-biased beat.

Marianne and Sharon's soul-searching quest has inspired others to begin to excavate their root identity, that unique seed-self, from the debris of neglect. None of them has any idea what it will take, where the journey will lead, or what will have to change. Nor do any of us. In fact you can never predict what chance encounter, what passing moment will propel you over the threshold and into an active relationship with the foreign territory of what your heart wants and is yearning for you to embody and express.

Nancy writes:

> At yoga class, the teacher announced that we would be focusing on opening our heart chakras that evening. Some postures consisted of expanding our upper chest forward and holding our shoulders back, and slowly circling our arms as we extended them from our arm sockets. By the end of class I felt very open, energized, and different in my body because I was no longer bending my shoulders forward to protect my heart.
>
> Two days later I was at work, where approximately 90 percent of the employees were women. As I walked through the lobby after lunch I noticed all the beautiful bouquets of flowers arriving for my coworkers. It was Valentine's Day and all the florists in town were converging on my workplace. I felt that every woman in the building would receive flowers except me. I could feel how much these men loved and appreciated the women in their lives. My emotions overwhelmed me—for the first time in my life, I realized on a deep level that some men truly love women. My reaction may sound strange to most people, but consider that I grew up in a family where my father displayed misogynistic feelings toward his wife and daughters.

On this Valentine's Day I was particularly feeling the loss of not having a special man in my life. For years I had been unconsciously shielding myself from love relationships because on some deep level I did not trust that a man could truly love me exactly for who I was. All these bouquets of flowers were challenging my belief system that said it was impossible for me to find true love.

I returned to my office with a tremendous sense of grief. Soon I started to have intense chest pains. The pain was so great that I could not breathe. Needless to say I was petrified. Although I was only thirty-two years old I feared that I was having a heart attack. Through my fears and tears I managed to make an emergency appointment with my doctor that afternoon. By the time I got to his office the pain had mostly subsided. I believe the opening of my heart during yoga cleared the channels for me to feel the emotional pain of that Valentine's Day more deeply. My body handled the intensity of that emotional pain by tightening the blood vessels around my heart, sending me a physical wake-up call.

Unsuspected by Nancy, her heart had been carefully nurturing her deeper identity—that of a woman capable of loving and wanting to experience being loved. *Sometimes the only way to awaken is to be flooded with the pain of not having what our heart is deeply yearning for.* Now Nancy must face learning how to love herself enough to say Yes to her wake-up call, a summons to claim what her heart knows about her wanting. Nancy must learn to believe that what her heart wants is within her realm of possibility.

HEART NOTES

Encountering the Essence of Your Wants

Our wanting may at first glance seem frivolous and immaterial, more a case of dissatisfaction or neediness than a heart-centered directive.

That's true when our wants are all lumped together like a flock of hungry sparrows, chirping to be fed and all looking alike. But when we sort through them we begin to see that there are distinct messages—some are more soulfully significant than we had noticed before. Take your journal and go to your favorite private spot.

- Sit quietly and turn your attention to your heart. Now relax into your breathing, and allow yourself to remember a time or an experience when you felt happy and at peace. Take the time to really remember the details and feel in your heart how happy you feel.

- Now imagine that you have taken a snapshot of this interior experience and know that you can return here at will. I call this Standing at the Altar of Your Heart. Do this each morning before you begin your day.

- Now write down a list of wants. Do not edit them. Let them pour out. If you become repetitious that's fine.

- Next take each item of your list to the altar of your heart and ask your heart if this is an important want. If it is not, delete it. If you can't decide, leave it alone. If one want seems to have special significance, star it for later.

- Now reduce your list to three items. This is the most difficult part of uncovering what your heart wants you to claim about yourself and genuinely love.

- Choose one item and pledge to make it happen. Ask your heart how to begin. Listen and then proceed. If you hear or feel nothing, don't give up. The next day repeat your question and continue to listen. The answer will come when you are ready to take the risk. There is no rush.

Half of the journey lies in your willingness to return again and again in your own behalf. Deep change has already begun by you making your list and distilling it to essence.

CHAPTER 6

What Your Heart Loves

This is what I ache for: intimacy with myself,
with others, with the world, intimacy that
touches the sacred in all that is life.
—ORIAH MOUNTAIN DREAMER

The human soul is a strong, abiding energy. We humans love deeply and fiercely and sometimes we love too long and too much, but always, at our very core, we love. We thrive when we feel intimately connected heart to heart and soul to soul. Those romantic images of love proffered by movies, novels, and television do not begin to touch the molten core of your heart's capacity to love. Or of your capacity to fiercely protect what you love. The fatal flaw in loving is that often we will sacrifice ourselves in order to give life to whatever we love. This is not always the best thing. Sacrificial love is devoid of intimacy, the heart's most hard-won gift.

If we reveal how deeply we are capable of loving we are often mocked or misunderstood. So we have to find other ways to express what comes from our heart and won't allow us to ignore its presence. Misguided, we will volunteer to give up or step aside from what we love in the misbegotten notion that we are being reasonable or sensible or grown up. We will make or buy icons or objects that we secretly know represent our loving, place them on our altars or in our pockets to remind us of the unspoken, the unclaimed, the unlived aspects of our loving energies. We make agreements that compromise our loving and then yearn for a miracle to rescue us from our own folly. We say, *I'll endure this loveless marriage until the children are grown,* or, *Mother won't live forever—after she dies then I'll begin my life or my painting or my own journey.* Without question, much of our authentic loving and our desire to be intimately engaged with life can lie languishing, waiting for the timing of another's life, another's permission.

Life is seldom presented in black-and-white choices. The heart knows that much of life resides in the grayness of the unlived life, the unexplored possibilities, whose promise is held by waiting, by our icons, the stories tearstained and privately etched on the pages of our journals or only spoken when we've had too much to drink or our despair gets to be too much to bear. Who among us does not wish to dare to love life fully and trust the wild and true energies of their heart? Yet we hesitate to step into the richly variegated grayness to discover the multiple tones of what is waiting to be uncovered. We fear that to speak honestly—without reservations—to ourself, about our one and precious life, is to disappoint others—to let someone, something, down. So we search for someone or something we can love more than we dare to love ourself, never realizing that we are creating a soul-numbing dishonesty.

What Is This Thing Called Love?

The story of Aphrodite, the Greek goddess of love, brings us closer to the multiple roots of love. Barbara Walker in *The Woman's*

Encyclopedia of Myths and Secrets introduces us to this goddess's genealogy of love. Her old name was Moira, and she was believed to be
older than time, with an unbroken lineage that sealed her relationship to the Fates and their covenant with Nature's mysteries exem-
plified by the Maiden, the Mother, and the Crone. She was known
across cultures by many names: Astarte; Stella Mara of the Sea; Hymen,
goddess of marriage; Ilithyia, goddess of childbirth; Venus, goddess
of sexuality and the hunt; and Androphonos, the Destroyer of Men.
During the Christian era her temple on the island of Cyprus was
converted to the temple of Mary. Revered by the Greeks, the
Romans, and the Egyptians (as Ay-Mari), she inspired one of the
greatest temples in Asia Minor to be dedicated to her worship.
Aphrodite was said to have mated with Semitic gods, affording her
a temple in Jerusalem. So many names, so many incarnations, so
many designations—thus we begin to uncover the nature of this
"thing" called love.

The Eskimos, in order to survive the many variations in their
frozen terrain, have dozens of words for snow—each describing a
particular quality, a certain necessary bit of information to ensure
survival. Surely in our culture, with love so all pervasive, we suffer
when we have only one word to describe that wilderness. *Love.*
There is the supposed endurance of parental love. The blood bond
of filial love, the tenuousness of romantic love, and the transparency
of narcissistic love that asks, "What have you done for me lately?"
And, if the answer is deficit, then such love is withdrawn and with-
held. There is the confusion among love and loyalty and deep affection and like and lust and on and on and on. There is even the
psychosis of "love at first sight," when sanity and reason dissolve
in the twinkling of a glance. There is love of country, of a new toy,
a dress, a song, your Mama's home cooking.

Aphroditic love is more familiar to the modern world as romantic love. It is certainly more expressive of the many variations of
romantic love when this energy is diffuse, unfocused, and not heart

centered. From this blurred perspective Aphroditic love represents the epitome of romantic love, full of angst and rapture but devoid of commitment and discipline, yet her mythology has other truths to tell, other lessons to teach. Aphroditic love is more than romantic love. She is also a Destroyer of Men. Do you know this quality of loving, when the tide turns and you feel filled with hatred for that which you once loved? Conversely, have you ever been so committed literally to something (not someone) that you would be willing to die to an old way, or relationship, rather than give up this inner conviction? Some would call this conviction a *cause* when they declare, "I would die for this," or "for my child, lover. . . ." But often we are speaking metaphorically, not literally.

There is a destroyer aspect of fierce love that comes into the foreground, compelling us to rid ourselves of anything that will impede authentic heart-centered love. Do you also know those times and places where you betrayed that which you deeply believed in and then died inside yourself? Do you remember those times when shame or fear of alienation killed your truth and you died a bit then, too? And can you remember the moment when you realized that you needed to betray that old contract with silence and speak out or this self-betrayal would sound a death knell in your soul? Destruction comes in many forms as it presents us with the unwanted knowledge that we must "destroy" what no longer holds vitality for our heart. And sometimes when we hold fast to the integrity that flows from our heart it seems we will be destroyed in the process.

Charles is a scientist who says he loves "my small patch of farmland. Only ten acres, it belonged to my father and his father before him. I feel I am the steward, the shepherd, the guardian, of this land." A very powerful developer began to buy up the surrounding land for a subdivision but couldn't close the deal without Charles's land. Charles said, "No." The developer countered first with money, then with threats, then with vandalism, and finally with fury. Charles's boss asked him to sell because of the adverse publicity, and still Charles would not yield. The local Businessmen's Association pleaded for the "good of all," that is, profit and capital gain, and Charles said, "No." In the end the developer and his power won out. The land was rezoned and Charles was evicted. Not a pretty story, nor a loving one. Love does not conquer all. Integrity is not to be bartered. But true love has a quality of integrity that nothing or no one can take away. The quality of this love is rooted in the integrity of the self, not a contest of will or a barter of relationship. A covenant with your own loving guarantees nothing save a connection to the integrity that resides within your heart and the release that comes when you know that you have not co-opted yourself with a lie. True love is fierce, it is enduring, and it can hurt.

Genuine love requires a depth of consciousness that at times you may find unbearable. Much of what you have assigned to your love basket may not be love at all. And if it is not love, then what is it that you feel?

HEART NOTES

Sorting the Seeds

This seed sorting will winnow out the chaff and leave you with the staff of the heart—love.

Get yourself plenty of newsprint or inexpensive paper, some pencils, a good eraser, and your mirror. Set aside an afternoon—some uninterrupted time—and place a glass of water and a box of Kleenex nearby. I am going to give you some sorting to do, if you have the heart for honest soul searching. Later I list some gradients of what you may have tossed into your love category.

- First write a pledge to yourself that you will not use this seed sorting to change anything. This is not about change; it is about putting your feelings in their proper place with integrity.

- Make a list of people and things that you absolutely love. Don't begin to second-guess yourself. This is a serious journey into the chambers of your heart and soul with deep respect for your body and your brain. You'll want both thought and feeling to contribute. Leave space between items so you can begin to sort out what you truly feel. Stop your list at twenty items so you don't overwhelm your intentions. You can add to it later.

- Now, using your mirror, look deeply into your eyes and ask these eyes if you are ready to be absolutely honest with yourself. And when you can say, "Yes," then proceed. Your results will only be as honest as you are honest.

- Taking each item on your list, test how you feel against each of the following gradients:

  Affection: Warm and satisfying mutuality

  Devotion: Commitment, either personal or transpersonal

  Infatuation: Shallow and without a sense of future

  Sexual Attraction: An affair of the genitals

  Narcissism: Loving being loved

  Appreciation: Empathy and shared mutuality

- Be sincere. Describe in your journal how many different ways you love. Do any of them surprise you, scare you, or please you? Write how you feel about getting to know yourself more intimately. Accept the depth of these insights and allow them to be strengths, not deficits. Please don't expect the world to teach you these precious things about yourself. Get busy, get real, do your own heart-centered work.

Relating to Love, Loving to Relate

Basic truth: We humans are relational beings. We wish to build community, not dissolve it. True, we seek independence and often settle for alienation. We lead with our hearts in a search for connection whether we realize it or not. Our sense of safety and self-worth is critically dependent upon feeling a sense of deep connection, of feeling valued and worthy. In today's mobile and transient society we find all manner of sensible and senseless ways to carry on as if moving from place to place, changing jobs and marriages and relationships is no big deal. We get the facts, use good sense, act like adults about our losses while keeping a tight lid on our sadness, our anxieties, our aloneness. As long as we are task oriented we can follow through.

Then there are those moments when the only way to continue is to repress what we are really feeling. Some of us do it with food, others with drugs, some with platitudes *(It's all for the best. I'll come through in the end. It'll all work out, I'm certain)*. And some with anger. Seldom do we face the great changes in our lives—the severing of friendships, the change of jobs, the loss of community—with honest truth. Who would listen? What can they do anyhow? What will they think? The biggest risk in our daily life is neither stress nor is it burnout. The biggest risk is *numb-out*.

Each and every time we say good-bye to or toss away something or someone that is carrying a bit of our heart's energy, our soul is participating in the loss, our dreams are remembering, and our ego is evaluating the personal cost. We don't alleviate the weight of these changes by being indifferent, resigned, or unconscious. Your mind may rationalize the losses by weighing the gains. Your ego may reassure you that everybody else is doing the same thing so buck up. Your food and liquor and credit card charges may prove that you have ways of soothing the emptiness or the loneliness or the disappointment, but your heart simply registers what you feel. If you can tune in to the wise counsel of your heart, it will convey your genuine feelings back to you in an attempt to wake you up to what really has meaning for you. Your heart will invite you to discover the strength of purpose and character you are capable of by bearing these losses consciously.

Harry, a fast-tracking executive says it best.

I had just arrived at my hotel after a pressured six weeks in which I sold my home, said good-bye to my friends, and accepted the envy and congratulations of my colleagues for this great promotion. So here I sat, a new city, no home yet, and as I looked at the phone book it hit me. There is no one, not one single person, in this city whom I know well enough to call and know they will be happy to hear from me. Nuts, so what. I'll make friends. I'll find another house. But I knew that I was avoiding the depth of my sadness about what I had agreed to give up. Not only the people, the relationships and the human community, but the familiarity of place and of ritual that affirms who I am and what I believe in. At that moment all I wanted was some familiar anything that I loved or that loved me—a smell, a touch, a voice. I wanted to be *home*.

Home carries a weight of embodied meaning whose roots begin in the memory of our first home, the womb. The memory of home—the images and the smells—stays with us into old age as a reminder of the comfort and calm that emanates from a place associated with loving remembrance. If our memories are tainted and devoid of sweetness, there is still a poignant pull, a wish or a regret for what never was. Your body is your soul's abode, and your heart will always receive you as the beloved resident that you are.

"Waking Down" to Self-Love

We humans continue to live as if we are solid earthbound mechanical forms while science collides with mysticism and announces, "Wake up! Wake up! You are an energetic radiance that is pulsing into and out of materiality many times a second." "Wake down! Wake down to the essential realm of your own being as you are dreamed into being, as your heart opens itself to the inspiration of Spirit, providing a ground upon which Soul can pitch her tent." Love pegs your tent to the bedrock of your heart space. To ignore your true feelings is not strength—it is not wisdom—it is not even good mental health. To ignore your feelings is to ignore who you are and what you know and love about yourself—to discount and devalue what is real and important to you and you alone.

We heal our losses, our relationships, and our wounded places by attending to the healing intentions of our heart. We can only honor the life and the embodiment of Spirit to the extent that we listen and honor our inner direction. If we cannot love ourself enough to listen to our innermost feelings with respect and compassion and even benevolent humor, we are deficit in our loving of others. We remain suspicious with chary disbelief when we are told that we are loved or valued or missed.

Dare we not care for our soul as compassionately as our heart cares for us? I invite you to listen to your heart's yearning to express love and yield to it, if not literally then at least symbolically as you are taught to deepen, to tap into the strong roots fed by the waters of soul. Your heart will teach what you love and provide you with insight into the reasons—many of which may be no surprise to you, since you have had thoughts or images that gave you a preview. The ordinary life lends us much more than structure and familiarity. All the fond bits and pieces afford nourishment, reflection, reassurance, homecoming. The old mug you always reach for to hold your morning tea, the view you have looked at all these many years out your kitchen window, the photo of yourself at four—all carry much more than just the obvious. Stop and inquire and see what you discover.

In her book, *Finding True Love,* Daphne Rose Kingma writes, "Everything worth having costs something, the price of true love is self-knowledge." If you wish to know *what* your heart loves, you will have to know and trust yourself even in the face of all the odds against what you believe is true for you. Access to this wisdom begins with uncovering what you love about yourself. Self-love does not mean being so self-absorbed that you feel the world rotates around you. Rather it means that you are ready to declare openly and without rancor what you value about yourself, in depth and with honesty. No embellishments, or apologies.

To love another more than you are able to love yourself renders you unable to voice the depth and breadth of your uniqueness. You are serving a false god—and heart and soul you pay the price by feeling uneasy and inauthentic. This inauthenticity will impede you from getting to the center of your own being without comparing what you find there with someone else's center. You cannot be real or true to your life's purpose because you have overshadowed it with the glow you attach to the other. Bit by bit you lose the desire to speak the intimate language of your truth. You mouth the words that you think would come out of the other's mouth or you believe the other wants you to speak. Everything about your life is in peril of becoming bogus and insubstantial.

Even those familiar protests—"I feel so selfish to speak my mind." Or the worst protest of all—"I dare not be me because my friends or family wouldn't understand." See—even this is not from the soul-searching depths of your integrity. This does not come from the heart. These are words with shallow roots, bereft of embodied impassioned meaning. Far better to speak from genuine feelings and hold yourself accountable for what spills forth. How can we ever receive love from another if we cannot love ourself? How can we ever discern words of truth and integrity if we do not voice them ourselves? Carl Jung says that we have turned our gods into symptoms—and deep down we feel the ache. Seneca says it best: "It is not because things are difficult that we do not dare; it is because we do not dare that they are difficult." Your heart's truth is daring.

HEART NOTES

Loving Yourself

Be daring and uncover the roots of your capacity for self-love.

- Take your journal and make a list with three headings:

  Things I would feel shy or stupid to admit touch my heart

  Ways I love secretly to avoid revealing my sensitivity

  Ways I disguise my love from others

- As you list items in each category, be specific and honest with yourself, without any explanations or excuses.

- Now take each item on your list and ask yourself, "If I were being true to myself how would I handle this? What is it I fear? Being foolish? Being different? Being all alone?"

- Read your responses and then turn to your heart and promise yourself you will make the changes that will allow you to be more open, more self-appreciative, and more self-loving—truer to yourself.

Daily, if you turn to your heart each time you have self-doubt or feel you have not loved yourself and ask for the strength to be heart centered, you will find this becoming a way of life—a life filled with meaning and a deep sense of loving, heart-centered affirmation.

True Love: Not Who But What

Understanding *who* you love defines how you wish to see yourself: what you wish to love about yourself but cannot yet lay claim to. We choose to love those whom we feel reflect back to us the best in ourselves. Even when the relationship turns sour and we feel we have made a wrong choice, there is still a lingering quality of regret that what we wanted the relationship to confirm is not to be found there. We love those human beings who offer us the affirmations we so hunger for. Or we are attracted to those human beings who will affirm our worthlessness. One way or another, those whom we love define how we wish to see ourselves—as good—or loving—or smart—or clever—or worthless.

Understanding *what* you love, however, defines what you are capable of becoming. When we invest our heart's energies only in superficialities, in materialism and acquisition, or in mimicking someone or something we admire, we risk living shallow lives. Skimming on the surface of great possibility, we cannot lay claim to our own depths until we are willing to go beyond the safety of the shallows. What you love symbolically reflects your spiritual genealogy—the thrust of your soul's evolution. Each and every thing you love is a variation of a single theme—each, a slightly different perspective of those qualities of soul you may be neglecting.

HEART NOTES

An Invitation

Now is the time to ask yourself honestly and openly what your heart loves.

- Find a quiet spot, turn off your cell phone and your telephone, light a candle, and take out your journal to note your responses.
- Do you know what your heart loves? Not who but *what*. What do you love or have a passion for, even though you may seldom or never do it? List these in your journal.
- How long, if ever, since you have inquired into what your heart yearns for?
- What is the one thing on your list you would do if you had no concern about harming or disrupting anything or anyone else?
- Now find a way to begin making this one thing happen in your life in any small way possible.

Do not be daunted by what may seem impossible or improbable. Your heart never yearns for the impossible or the improbable—that's the ego's role. Your heart is absolutely attuned to your soul's purpose, and it carries the energetic intentions that will lead you forward on your journey. Remember the journey of a lifetime begins with a single purposeful step. Conscious heart-centered intention will lead you to an open door you have never noticed before. Stepping even one step through that opening can be life saving.

Healing the Past

Sandra tells her story about decades of being unable to love herself because of an event in her early adulthood and the healing that occurred when suddenly a "door" opened where before there had only been a wall.

> When I was a young college student, aged twenty, I became pregnant, left college, and had a baby, a healthy girl, and after much agonizing I gave her away for adoption. I was self-supporting, working my way through college, and had no resources to give my daughter what I wanted her to have in life. I returned to college and on the surface resumed what appeared to be a normal life.
>
> I went on to earn three college degrees including a Ph.D. and had much success in my career. However, my heart always, always yearned for the tiny baby girl that I could only view through the nursery window and was never allowed to touch. I yearned to know how her life had been, was she okay, did she have a good life, was she even alive. There was always a part of my heart that felt empty, and I tried in many ways over the years to fill this space.
>
> I entered therapy ten years ago to face the pain in my heart of giving away my daughter. I began an active search for her.

Facing the pain helped, and though the emptiness in my heart was still there, it was no longer driving my actions.

Recently, in the midst of a major transition with my professional life, my daughter and I found each other. Rather, she found me through the agency that arranged her adoption. The greatest sorrow in my heart has now become my greatest joy. After our initial, very intense and emotional meeting, we continued frequent contact, sharing stories and getting to know each other.

As we have talked, we are now aware that we were looking for each other from our heart space for all these years. We knew in our hearts that we had to find each other to get our questions about the past answered. We both acknowledge that a part of our lives is now complete, our questions answered, and our hearts are at peace in a way we have never known before. I am convinced that by listening to this "heart energy" we found each other at the perfect time in our lives and that the heart connection we shared from the time of her birth led us to each other. We were ready to meet and know each other. I have great reverence for this heart knowledge as it has brought me incredible peace and joy.

Transforming Fear and Doubt into Self-Love

Writer Oriah Mountain Dreamer reminds us of how difficult it is to follow our deepest desires: "Each time I follow my deepest desires, fear is there wringing her hands, cautioning me with her litanies of what-ifs." Calling upon your heart's strength and wisdom, you must dare to wash your hands of bending to fear's incantations if you are to live a love-centered life. To deny that fear resides within you is foolhardy; instead face into your fears and search their pockets for the truth. Fear steals a small grain of self-doubt and bakes it into a meal, and we swallow her offering whole, never questioning the roots of our hunger or fear's intent. Fear will disintegrate into that single grain of truth when permeated by your heart's fiercely radiant love.

The things we love carry the representations of our desires, our sorrows, our strengths, and our betrayals. All too often we reach for the object or the acquisition that deep in our heart we know carries that bit of our life we are unwilling or unable to meet face to face. And then we go unconscious, as if the symbol itself will do the work of remembrance. Each remembrance begs to be integrated. How are you different, more real, truer to yourself, when you integrate the energy carried by each symbol? What if you accepted the capacity of your heart to soften easily and fully whenever you feel as you felt when your eyes fell upon this object and you claimed it for your altar? Dare to remember this moment and the joy it brought you fully, and then find that heart-filled energy elsewhere in your life.

Each symbol or acquisition is an invitation to dive deeply and ask yourself, "What is my soul trying to tell me about myself—what in my life am I devaluing by not allowing the energies behind this object to come alive and take its place in my consciousness?"

How often in the course of your day do you ever meet yourself—your undisguised, honest true self? Do you like her? Can you love her and what she loves as ferociously as her heart and soul love her? When you can, then you will be ready to live your one and precious life fully.

HEART NOTES

Step by Step

We find that when we do not have the heart for the difficult things in life, our soul lies languishing and life trudges on. Even on the most difficult of days this need not be the case. When the morning breaks, or the hour arises that you feel you are unable even to trudge, try this contemplative walking prayer. You will find your heart expand with the vitality that comes from an intimate appreciation of the ordinary.

- Begin to walk by raising your head and fixing your eyes on an object straight ahead.

- Walk toward it, and as you do so note each object you pass and give thanks for that energy. If you have associations to it, or history with it, give thanks for that.

- Do this every time you find yourself slipping into self-doubt or despair. Walk and express your gratitude to each space, each place, each object.

- When you are ready, go outside and take a longer walk while doing the same contemplative acts of recognition and appreciation.

Evidence of your reason for living, your reason for being is right here, tucked within the places and spaces that surround you. Take a walk and consciously allow yourself to be walked—walked by the vitality of recognition and gratitude. Step by step, you will find your way.

CHAPTER 7

Where Your Heart Lives

Hope is the thing with feathers
That perches in the soul.
—EMILY DICKINSON

In a tale of the West the cowboy is overheard saying, "I'm sure enuff homesick for my own little spread," and an onlooker muses, "There's no accountin' for what some folks call home. I just guess home is where your heart is."

If home is where the heart lives, then what special something draws your heart there? Let's tilt our question a bit. Remember, it's the way of the deep feminine to notice connections, savor metaphors, and see similarities. This energy is especially drawn to relationships, to what matches or seems related to something else. So another way to explore where your heart lives is to ask, "Where does my heart feel most connected, become most lively? Are there spaces and places where its beat quickens, or deepens, and I just know *this is home*?"

The experience can be sudden and inexplicable. Or it can creep up on you slowly and steadily until you and it are one, or you can feel overtaken by the headlong full-body pitch into the recognition that *this, this* is so right for me. The experience moves through you like the words of a poem that bring tears to your eyes and you realize you are weeping for a part of your unexplored life. Or, you've touched a place within that has been avoided but is more you than you ever realized before, a place of prayer and possibility. Maybe there is a piece of music that shifts your imagination, putting you in contact with a part of yourself that is alive and vital and seldom if ever called upon. And there are those times, when wandering through the vast reaches of the imagination, an inner terrain appears before your eyes as you come upon a place that so suits your heart that you know, body and soul, you are *home.*

Knowing You Are Home

I remember the first time I went, under protest, to live in Central America. As I stepped off the ship's gangplank and into the sultry, heavy air laden with the scent of flowers I could not yet name bursting from canopies of the greenest green I had ever seen, I knew I had come *home.* The resonance of recognition was first in my body. I noticed it in my walk as my gait loosened and I felt my entire body following the pulse of the Earth. *Ah,* I thought, *how close I almost came to missing this; I belong here.* Now, years later, I have only to cross the southernmost border, or play Latin music, or visit my favorite Cuban restaurant and I feel that precious sense of homecoming once more. And it is bittersweet, because I cannot live there now. Not literally. Eventually I had to return to where my family and professional life are. However, I have taught myself how to carry the vitality I found there within my imagination and through the music, food, and languages I surround myself with at home. We can't always literally live where our heart is vitalized, but we must learn to recognize the qualities it holds and recreate them as best we can.

To ignore the cellular shifts that occur within our body when we set foot on a certain soil or glimpse a particular place that sets off an internal resonance of "home" prevents us from listening to the deep body wisdom that knows what and where our deeper sense of well-being—of Soul—is rooted. It is never a matter of changing your life in order to move or travel or reinvent yourself. This kind of challenge is daunting for most of us. We do not have to literalize the change. Once we recognize the resonance, we can recreate it in our imagination or consciously create a small but meaningful part of what home is to us wherever we actually live, like the music and the Cuban food I so enjoy. The deeply embodied sense of home is a matter of heart. It is a commitment to listening, viscerally and cellularly, to what moves you, what feeds your deepest hungers, and taking that very seriously. Once you recognize and claim the feeling with all its accompanying affect, it is possible to recreate it, if only in your imagination, no matter where or how you live. Not in a fantastic or frivolous way, as if you were playing some fantasy game or fooling yourself into believing something that is not real. Instead you, and you alone, must learn how to believe these deeper truths about yourself and claim them as an integral part of your soul's journey, whether they make sense to anyone else or not. What you know with your heart cannot be denied without losing a part of your soul. Sometimes we first have to wade through the shadow side of our relationship with our heart's wisdom before we are free to be who we truly yearn to be. We can discover this shadow side's energy when we are faced with our own denial.

Marilyn tells us of the cost of denial.

After a trip to Mexico I returned home full of plans to create a sunroom reminiscent of the patio where I had sat during one sunset evening. I returned filled with the exquisite joy I felt as the Mexican sky turned apricot and then mauve deepening into purple-gray. Surrounded by the colors and the warm breeze I felt a profound sense of walking into and being "colored" by the hues. I don't know how long I sat, immersed in the vibrating silence and held by a sense of homecoming. When my tears finally ceased I realized I had been crying with joy. Joy? Yes, and for no discernible reason other than the pure splendor of this sunset and the immense sense of filling my heart to overflowing. *I want my inner life to be colored by these colors,* I thought. *What on earth does that mean? Well, I don't know exactly but I am determined to make it happen.* The next day I found a scarf in the Mexican crafts market swirled, splashed, infused with those sunset colors so I bought it, in remembrance. *Allow me to keep my heart open and full, infused with this blessing, this energy,* I prayed.

Once home, the vacation clothes washed and put away, the luggage stored, I draped my scarf across my altar and plunged into my daily life. That first morning, having breakfast in my old familiar sunroom I noticed the colors. Cheery yellow and clean blue and white. *I have always liked this room,* I thought, *and it is not at all like the "Mexican" colors of my heart.* I remember that with that thought I felt both a sense of excitement and a series of little thumps in my chest. Like someone or something is knocking at my rib cage. I laughed and then said, seriously, *I hear you and I won't forget.* But forget I did. It was too much work to repaint the sunroom. My partner teased me that I'd have to become a Key West "Parrot Head" (a Jimmy Buffett fan) if I was going to create some faux Mexican sunset-splashed haven. Well, I don't know about the Buffett part, but the faux part rang hollow and embarrassed me, so I let my intention be diminished along with my heart's desire. After all it was probably only a vacation moment—and a sensible life isn't lived according to sunsets and fantasies—is it?

Then a curious thing occurred. My mother sent me a tie-dyed tee shirt that I had worn during high school. She said she thought she had completely emptied all the bureau drawers but this mysteriously appeared. The colors? Yes, apricot, mauve, and purply blue. Then I turned a corner in my kitchen too fast and whacked my thigh on the edge of an open cabinet door. That evening I noticed it was turning mauve and purple and blue— quite striking against the remainder of my apricot tan. Again my heart leaped up and thumped three tiny knocks against my chest. When I went to bed that night I knew I had betrayed myself. My heart was leading me to create a space where I could discover my purpose as a woman, as a human being, as a soulful being, and I allowed it to be dismissed as *faux*.

When my heart held up a mirror of my soul I felt the image shimmer within every cell and the shimmer was apricot and mauve and purply blue. I shrouded that mirror, dulled those colors with words and reason, dashing my heart's sense of place onto the rocks of practicality. Now it was up to me to gather the shards and take my heart more seriously than I have ever taken anything before this knowing; or suffer the grief of turning away from the most authentic chapel I will every enter. A chapel of the true me—the spiritually guided me.

Each of us carries a picture of a heart-centered "home" in our imagination. We express it by the things we feel drawn to but put off acquiring or doing or creating. You'll recognize the signs whenever you hear yourself saying, "I always wanted to do . . . ," or, "Someday I'm going to do . . . ."

For myself, I know that if I die without learning to speak Spanish well a part of my heart will never have been served. For Spanish is not only a lovely lyrical language, it is tasty as I speak, it delights my sense of quickening vitality, it lends me a keen sense of homecoming.

HEART NOTES

Catching a Glimpse of Your Heart's Sense of Home

This is a playful, creative way to allow your heart to guide you toward creating a deeper, more meaningful home—one that reflects and evokes your heart-centered uniqueness. This will be especially meaningful if you are thinking about a "dream" home, or job, or vacation, or partner. You can chose a category or make a general book of favorite colors or textures or destinations.

- Make or buy a scrapbook to hold clippings, photos, drawings, and anything else you can find that reflects what your heart yearns for.
- As you make each choice, check it out with your heart to be certain it is correct.
- Be selective. If the picture or poem is almost but not quite right, alter it. Cut and paste a collage or write your own verse; do all you are able to do to create a reflection of your heart's truth.
- Now read your book from cover to cover and write what your heart is showing you that you love.

The first step toward accepting your heart's guidance is focused recognition. If you don't recognize the opportunity when you are in its presence, you won't know how to live a more authentic life even if the opportunity is right before your eyes. You may begin this scrapbook on a weekend, but it is far more than a weekend project. I have known people who do this project for every major change in their lives. Your heart fills your life with clues about how to live a vital and renewing life. Yearning is a wake-up call. Allow yourself to go slowly and thoughtfully as you sort out your yearnings.

Pausing to Catch Up with Ourself

How infrequently do most of us pause and realize that the outer terrain that resonates so deeply is a reflection of the inner one that is calling, calling. I, like many others, have always been led by a paradoxical set of energies that draws me toward a community in which I can feel welcome, safe, and related, but also independent and able to find time and permission to be by myself. When a place "speaks to me," it usually has one or more of these qualities—the qualities of community, shared purpose, and individual personal space. My favorite rhythm is to go to bed with the hum of voices weaving in and out of conversation in a nearby room. As a child my bedroom was above the kitchen, and I loved to hear the soft rise and fall of the adults' voices in their after-dinner banter as I drifted off to sleep. Complete solitude is not my way—nor is highly extroverted camaraderie. Knowing these things has helped me make choices that for the most part have been very satisfying.

HEART NOTES

Discovering Your Way

Do you know your way? What are the inner rhythms that allow you to feel at ease, at home, among others? What helps you to recognize this? Answering this question will allow you to reduce the stress in your life. Stress is like a dripping faucet. After a while you adjust to the interruption, but at what cost to your inner sense of quietude, of order? Stress disrupts the physical body, and even more important, it blurs your natural heart-centered rhythms so that you become fatigued and impatient. For most women and a good number of men, fatigue and depression are Siamese twins—the prolonged presence of one summons the presence of the other.

This exercise will help you minimize fatigue and depression and maximize well-being. You will want your journal and a quiet place to sit and reflect.

- List your favorite life rhythms (quiet reflection, out alone in Nature, talking with a close friend, at the seashore, hiking, . . .) in your journal.
- Now list how you recognize when a rhythm is deeply satisfying.
- How can you increase those that satisfy and begin to eliminate those that stress you?
- Choose a way you can apply this recognition of your preferred rhythm to your daily life and record what changes.
- Check how your sense of inner rhythm was at work. If the outcome didn't work, see if you can identify what went against your rhythm.

You may find this exercise difficult to do, because I am asking you to trust that what you think is merely a whim is truly a message from your heart's wisdom. If you feel lost, recall your favorite fairytale character. Describe his or her rhythms—bold, quiet, in the center of a family, independent? Begin here.

Your Way in the World

Some of us are visual, and for us the appearance of a place is primary. Others are olfactory, where fragrances and smells evoke an inner affirmation. Then there are those of us who are tactile and seek certain textures, certain temperatures. We move through life finding home via our fingertips—our touch. Slipping into a pond or ocean, sliding into a silky garment, allowing the soft caress of a bubble bath to move across our skin awakens a deeper sensibility. It is up to you to know yourself well enough to recognize these unique thresholds so that you can follow where your heart wants to lead you, into a deeper and more intimate relationship with yourself.

Then there is a geography known only to your heart, for which there are no maps. We enter this terrain of the heart when we meditate or step into the geography of our imagination. We know we are home because our respiration smoothes out and we perceive sounds and smells and a fragrance of homecoming. *Chronos* time, that linear ticking of the clock, ceases to have meaning, and the pressure of time falls away. At every turn there is beauty. Here we are imbued with joy, wrapped in the exquisite spiral of belonging. At every return we are welcomed as the beloved, and we feel every molecule of our being sighing with the sweet rapture of this welcome. Your heart lives in a spiritual realm deeply connected to caverns and chambers and labyrinths of which your ego knows nothing. The opportunity to recognize and accept the invitation to cross this threshold can appear without any preamble, with no warning at all.

One rainswept night in the south of Spain a group of women and I were hurrying to an out-of-the-way restaurant whose culinary reputation was well known. As we dodged the high coastal winds and rain flurries, my companion motioned for me to follow her. She cut off at a sharp angle and in no time we had left the cheerful chatter of our group behind and were moving quickly toward the unsheltered breakwater. The clouds were ragged with the high wind, and the moon paved the ebb tide with a glimmering pathway into the distant inky darkness. Intent upon my footing I stopped in midstride when I chanced to glance up to locate my companion and saw *home*. Maybe it was five minutes or even only five seconds that my glance hung in the balance—I don't know because clock time ceased as I stepped into the timelessness of the heart. *Kairos* time—the eternal beat of the sacred. There across the water stood the exposed foundations of the Temple to Venus/Astarte. Usually submerged, the conjunction of time and tide were such that it was exposed, and the moon pointed a path that uncounted numbers of women had once walked as they went to pay homage to their Goddess-self. My body felt their presence and the quiet anticipation they must have felt. The scene filled my body with a sense of complete familiarity and relaxation. My heart had found a home. I knew this pathway, and I could feel the joy and the tears of those pilgrims palpable and present. I have no memory of thinking this—no sense of history or story that told me where I was or what I was seeing. Only the swelling of my heart in recognition of this homecoming. The sky darkened as clouds covered the moon, and the path to the temple disappeared in a single unraveling motion as if it was being reabsorbed into the past. My friend and I returned to the cobbled street that led to the restaurant without saying much. Words were superfluous. We had been home and heart to heart we knew it.

Coretta writes:

> Thomas had chided me, with a smile and nicely, about never wanting to go with him to his dance club. "Come on," he'd say, "loosen up and at least let the music get under your skin." I always would brush him off—I had never been much of a dancer and I was loathe to go make a spectacle of myself at seventy. It was Saturday afternoon—rainy and a slow, gray-coated day when out of a perverse sense of teaching Thomas to stop annoying me I agreed to go with him to his club. They will all be younger than we, more supple, practiced. *It won't take him long to recognize how silly his insistence really is,* I thought.
>
> As we entered I could hear the strains of "Has Anybody Seen My Gal?" An unusually warm feeling flooded my breast. Me? I'm five foot two and even though my eyes are brown the quick beat and the familiar melody seemed unexpectedly welcoming. There was no halting the tumble of memories—the dance pavilion at the beach every summer—the dances and the summer suppers and the laughter and yes, something more—just beyond memory but ever so precious. What? I couldn't quite grasp it but I knew I was about to embarrass myself by crying so I rushed to the bathroom.

Then I remembered an old conversation, shared every summer for years, between my best friend and me. How long ago? Thirty-five, forty years? "Remember when I'm an old lady I want you to promise to put my rocking chair facing the pavilion so I can hear the music and watch the fireflies dance to the beat. Promise?" And we'd laugh and swear to do this for one another. When Dorrie died, so did these memories, as if without her they held no meaning, no promise.

My heart racing I wondered, *How can I ever go home again?* There is no pavilion any more—only a shopping mall and a parking lot. *Stop this foolishness,* I told my heart. *Behave yourself!* Washing my face and hands I went reluctantly back to where I had left Thomas. As I approached he said, "Come on, give it a whirl—be young with me!!" And then I knew that my heart loves the music, the remembrance of summers past and the promise of summer yet to arrive. Be young with me, it sings, be young with me. Let's go home again.

I went into the dance club an older woman who had forgotten Dorrie and where my heart is always waiting to meet me. I left, that same older woman yet infused with a sense of having crossed a forgotten threshold and stepped into a heart space, into home.

Remembrance does take us home again. Our body does not discriminate between the actual event and the remembered one. A warm feeling is a warm feeling, leaving the body gently touched by endorphins, by the healing and soothing release of hormones and the pleasures of the experience. A memory can chill you to the bone or fill you with warmth and cause you to smile involuntarily. When the heart recognizes where it lives, all is right in the interior world. Your heart knows what matters most to you. Your heart knows where and with what memories you are closest to its profound love for you.

The Soul's Terrain

Then there are those times when your heart is touched, awakened, by the profound sense of arrival at your soul's terrain in a dream. My friend Bob tells us this story.

> In his wonderful book, *The Alchemist,* Paulo Coelho quotes an important message of the heart. "Be aware of the place where you are brought to tears. That's where I am and that's where your treasure is." The quote, reminds me of a dream-gift I received on a wondrously clear Canadian night during a Vision Quest in 2000.
>
> I dreamed it was my task to ascend to the heavens to collect stars that I would distribute to people on earth. I wrapped them in white paper and distributed them twelve to a box. While packing a box I was awakened by four raindrops falling on my face. The final cold drop fell on my bottom lip and I tasted it with delight. But then I noted that there wasn't a cloud in the sky. I checked my sleeping bag and it was completely dry. I fingered the leaves on the bush alongside my nest. I got up and walked around my circle with a flashlight. Everything was dry.
>
> A bit quizzical, I crawled back into my bag to study the most glorious sky I had ever seen. I glanced to my left and saw my first-ever falling star. Then quickly a second star fell. About a minute later a third star went cascading down, and a voice asked, "Is that enough?" Surprised at my own brazenness, I replied, "One more, please." And there it was. My heart was in my throat and it unlocked a flood of tears that washed my starry eyes. I was at the threshold and I knew clearly where my treasure is.

Carl Jung, the Swiss psychiatrist who spent his life exploring the dreaming psyche, wrote, "The utterances of the heart—unlike those of the discriminating intellect—always relate to the whole. . . . What the heart hears are the great things that span our whole lives, the

experiences which we do nothing to arrange but which we ourselves suffer."

Too often we do our utmost to avoid that which brings us to
tears. Yet Jung's words remind us that the experiences that take us
by surprise, sometimes causing us to tear up or even weep with
wrenching sobs, are not to be brushed aside. These experiences hold
the clues to our infinite yearning. Within the span of every life there
is a desire to seek and follow an inner vision—a quest—a destiny.

How often have you described yourself by describing the geography of your bodysoul? *I'm an ocean person. Salt and sea are essentially
where I live*—or, *I'm definitely a city person, I love the early morning hours
before the concrete and glass comes alive with the buzz and hum of humanity.* The descriptions of this geography sketch out the metaphors that
feed your soul and give voice to your heart. Body and soul, there
are some experiences, images, and memories that are nutrient and
others that, no matter how lovely, offer no sustenance at all.

Nutritionists and indigenous people tell us that our body thrives
on the foods and the environment of our birthplace. The memory
of those nutrients resides at a cellular level. The rhythms and the
smells and the temperatures and even the cadences of these experiences are deeply imprinted. Like Coretta's music, they are under our
skin, in our bellies and our hearts.

When we are yearning for this "food" and are unaware of what
it is that is calling to us, we will eat and drink and shop and still feel
sadly empty and loving ourself less. There is nothing more confusing and self-defeating then unconscious gobbling. Desire turns into
despair and despair into self-hatred. Then your heart's voice is dulled,
extinguished, or takes on a Medusa quality that turns you to stone.
You don't know where you live or even at times what is worth
living for.

Exploring Your Heart's Geography

Do you know where your heart lives? Start with the sort of place or space that lifts your spirits and causes your bodysoul to sing.

- Make a list of the times or the experiences where you have felt completely at ease with yourself. Write them in your journal.
- Now review them and write down what was special about each one. You will probably find there is a definite pattern or many similarities.
- Relax and, one by one, take each one into your heart space. Allow yourself to remember the specialness and ask your heart if this is home.
- Star the ones that are heart places.
- Now, ask yourself, "How often do I consciously recreate this sense of spiritual homecoming for myself?"
- And if not, why not?

Choose intentionally to *go home* at least once a week for the next six months and see how much closer you feel attuned to your deep feminine—to that inner environment that is always seeking to find compatibility with the external environment. If you cannot make the journey literally, then make it symbolically by using your imagination. Hannah's heart sings when she is at the seashore at dawn. She yearns for the summertime and her annual trip. These days she gets up once a week, puts on her beach clothes—her white tee shirt, soft pants, and a jacket—and goes to the "beach" in her imagination as she watches the sun rise. On these mornings she makes a pot of coffee and sits at a table in her sunroom remembering what her heart loves. She is committed to not feeling sad. Instead she allows herself to savor that although she lives in the city, her heart can sing with the memory of sunrise at the beach and her body is fed by the ritual. As she dresses and steps out of her home on her way to another day in the office, she pledges to be the Hannah of the Beach. This Hannah knows herself and further, she likes herself. Be your own Hannah. You'll know what to do and how to do it. Set a table in the sanctuary of your heart space. Go home and have a meal of soul food.

What Feeds Your Heart When It Is Home?

Macusa fell in love with Portugal. What a total surprise. The trip was a company award for outstanding sales support. A once-in-a-life-time opportunity. And she fell in love with—well, with what exactly? This is an important question. *What exactly?* Macusa spent days wishing she could return and then she spent weeks grieving because she felt she never would. Instead of savoring and cultivating what she had discovered about herself she began to let her fear of being separated forever color her life, casting a pall over everything. Then one day she came across a tiny bottle of olive oil she had picked up at a favorite restaurant as she was leaving for the last time. The words she spoke then came back to her in a flash, and she was taken aback by their wisdom. She had turned to the owner of the restaurant and said, "When I get home I will buy this oil and every time I use it or see the bottle I will be here once more and as happy as I have been with the *freedom* of spirit I have found here in your beautiful country." *Freedom of spirit. Home. Home,* no matter where Macusa lives or works, her heart can take her there. *Home* is not a place or a space or a condition. *Home* is a way of being, deeply connected to your heart's wisdom and guidance.

Not enough, your ego cries. *I have been settling for crumbs and dregs and leftovers all my life. I want the whole thing not some poor substitute. I don't want to sample life I want to live it!* We are not talking about settling here. We are talking about knowing the difference between authenticity, who you genuinely are, and what you feel you have to acquire or achieve in order to live your uniqueness. You are settling for crumbs when you deny your heart's wisdom that teaches you how to live from the depths of your soul outward no matter where you are. Unrequited yearning, bitterness, and feelings of deprivation and dissatisfaction harm the immune system and severely limit the range of our creative responses to life. We look in the mirror and refuse to love the face we see before us. We get up each morning and regret what we don't have without ever claiming what is within and ours alone. When you follow your heart's guidance you will find you are never alone, never without possibility, never left with just crumbs.

Shalette writes that she has always dreamed of going to China.

It has definitely been a heart's desire. I come from a poor background. No college, no money, and no way to do much more than live from month to month. My one pleasure has been in collecting and planting cuttings from my friend's gardens. Many a morning as I work in my garden I dream of China and cry bitter tears because I am so damn poor I have to scrape and save just to go to the beach every two years. And not a great vacation either. I stay in a borrowed cottage and have to fend against mosquitoes, mice, and flies. But I always look forward to the time away.

I have a part of my backyard I've given up on. Too many brambles and weeds and work. About ten years ago I planted four hydrangeas there and they happily grow, covered with their gay bright blossoms, thriving on my neglect.

Well, a strange thing happened and I discovered the answer that was right under my nose all along. I was sighing to a friend that it had rained so much for the last two years that my garden couldn't yield the lovely bouquets that were my one guaranteed pleasure in life. Startled she said, "What are you talking about? You have the most beautiful hydrangeas I have ever seen."

"Hydrangeas aren't flowers to cut and enjoy—they are just big blue blobs," I huffed. "They go against nature—blue is sky and sea not flowers!"

The next day when I went out to get my paper there was a big parcel on my front steps with this note: "Please accept this vase, it belonged to my mother who brought it back with her after she had spent ten years as a missionary in China. The cloth is to go beneath it and the book is self-explanatory." Inside was a beautiful cloisonné vase and a handmade linen cloth appliquéd with the most delicate birds and flowers. Their beauty took my breath away. I immediately began to think that I didn't have anywhere in my house worthy of such beauty. Everything is so plain, so shabby by comparison. These thoughts caused a pang to strike my heart and I knew I had to stop my remorse and enjoy what I had just been given. The book was a beautifully illustrated book about tiny Chinese shrines, gardens, and flower arrangements. I was halfway through it when I suddenly realized that every other one had some form of hydrangea blossom in it! There—here— in my abandoned backyard my bit of China has been thriving, waiting for me to discover it. My heart leapt with such joy! I felt I was going to faint and then I laughed and cried and sang. Now you may or may not believe this, but once I got it that my heart lives with the beauty of China no matter where I am, I began to redo where I actually live. Today the cloth and vase sit on my old wooden kitchen table, which has been transformed by three coats of blue lacquer. One by one each room has been made as simple and as lovely as time and heartfelt caring can make it. All summer long I have hydrangeas in the house—even in my bathroom. I call them my heart blossoms. And in the winter I have dried bouquets as a reminder that spring will come again. My heart knew the day would come when my life would change if only I would step into the neglected part of my life and rediscover China.

Vision Questing

Soul searching, the inner quest for home, usually originates in the depths of one's very being. The vision quest is a ritual of focused preparation in order to cleanse the body and the mind and open the heart to a healing vision. The initiate agrees to fast, to follow her dreams, and to enter a sweat lodge for prayer and meditation prior to setting herself apart from the community so she can hear Spirit speak to her from the depths of her being about her life's purpose. Every step of this age-old ritual is designed to assist the participant in leaving behind the false attachments to materiality and ego identity and stepping from clock time *(Chronos)* into sacred time *(Kairos)* when she enters the sacred circle of the sweat lodge. Since time immemorial we humans have sought ways to step beyond the limits of our flesh and minds and enter into a nature-centered relationship with the rhythms of soul. We have touched the hem of the garments of Eternity through prayer, ecstatic dance, great poetry, deep meditation, and life-threatening illness. Sorrow and loss have beckoned us there; still we seek not only participation but a dialogue—a sense of an embodied love relationship with soul. The vision quest is one such avenue into a partnership with the spirit of Nature—with the intention of creation. Here Nature embraces you at every turn. First, as you fast, your body is cleansed of the distractions of hunger and the unnatural toxins of food. We go against our own nature eating and drinking substances that nourish neither our body nor our soul. Next we are invited to ask for a dream before sleeping that will guide and prepare us on our quest. These dreams are shared with the group once you have entered the circle of the sweat lodge.

As the flap at the entrance of the sweat lodge is lowered, you are plunged into absolute heat and darkness. The only orientation you have is to the glow of the heated coals in the fire pit at the center of your circle and the touch of the earth beneath your seated body. The steam from the cold water the shaman pours upon the coals enhances your sweating as you pray for those you are with.

You must enter a sweat lodge on your hands and knees—only one step above the posture you took when you entered this world. You enter stripped of all jewelry, eyeglasses, and superfluous clothing. Empty of stomach, it is time to empty your mind and listen to your heart. You are instructed to open your heart and pray for others. This will distract your ego from its concerns, redirecting your energies so they come from a deeper, less externally oriented reservoir, which will strengthen your own ability to "take the heat." When the ritual ends you emerge disoriented and lightheaded. In many ways your spiritual compass is being realigned. In the total blackness and the intense heat the polar light of your prayers awakens your ego's respect for the immense potency that steadily emanates from your heart. As you lie upon the cool earth you allow your consciousness to slowly re-inhabit your body by following your heart's lead.

The ritual is one of letting go of the superfluous—the unnecessary—in order to strip down to the basics of your life. Setting aside all the interruptions, schedules, and commitments, you face into your fears and your desires, creating an opening for your true self to visit you and to speak. You may enter the sweat lodge with hesitation and even fear, but once you are willing to surrender to the ritual you begin to realize how much of your life is spent in unconscious activity—without heart.

Because of the heat every participant must have a doctor's release in order to participate in a sweat. The heat and the intensity can affect your body if you have respiratory or circulation problems. Curiously enough, the surrender to the process is also healing for the body, since it cleanses the body of toxins through sweating and releases stress through prayer and meditation.

Creating your own heart-centered place of ritual is just as healing. A garden niche, a small room beautifully and sparingly furnished, a lovely spot in your home—the list can be long—the effect incalculable if it creates a heartfelt sense of home.

Pilgrims Along the Way

From the poet, author, and world traveler Phil Cousineau's book, *The Book of Roads,* comes this story of unexpectedly visiting a place of heart and meeting another pilgrim seeking the way.

Streams of sunlight stream through the stained glass windows. My heart surges as I enter the ancient labyrinth. Each step I take slows time as I follow the ancient winding way over the white flagstones. Each step on the path has been worn smooth by pilgrims over the last eight hundred years. A strange tension builds as the turns tighten and I close on the center, then slip inside, as if in a dream.

A cool clarity comes over me. The knot inside me begins to loosen. The voices in the cathedral fade away and I hear nothing but the sound of my own blood surge. I feel a rare and utter stillness, as if poised on the still point of the world.

Slowly, I follow the meandering path back out of the labyrinth. As I emerge, an old Frenchman in a black felt beret is waiting. He taps me on the arm with the crook of his oak cane. He has the eyes of a court jester, the wariness of a wayward pilgrim. With the riddling power of a traveling bard, he asks me, "Do you know where I can find God?"

I feel a cool shiver down my spine, a peculiar prickling at the back of my neck. His eyebrows arch expectantly. Is he a mad theologian? A sardonic existentialist? Could he be testing my knowledge of arcane architecture or medieval philosophy? He squints, waits impatiently, as if there are words lurking in me that might surprise us both.

Suddenly a ray of blue light slants from the brilliantly bright rose window above the choir loft and finds my face, warms my soul.

Only now do I realize I've been waiting for this question all my life. I point my right thumb over my shoulder, indicating the whorling pattern in the stone floor. . . .

HEART NOTES

Making a Heart-Centered Pilgrimage

Stress often awakens us in the middle of the night, its icy agitated grasp pulling us from the sanctuary of our heart, making our sweet matter feel alien and uninhabitable. When you awaken in the middle of the night filled with dread or anxiety, it is often a summons to listen to your heart telling you how you are not living your life in accord with your soul's purpose. Instead of responding to the symptoms or the racing thoughts, you can use this opportunity to create a pilgrimage for yourself—a heart-centered journey.

- Place your journal, a pen, and a flashlight next to your bed to have on hand when you are awakened.
- When you are awakened, ask your heart what you are avoiding about your own destiny, your own passion, your truth.
- Listen and trust the answer, even though it may come to you as an image, a sensation, a memory, or some other subtle language.
- Write your "conversation" down to honor it and record this more creative heart-guided way of getting to know yourself more intimately.

Asleep, our emotions usually reflect the messages of the deep unconscious that in our waking hours we cannot discern. We can treat these emotions as hostile and frightening, or we can welcome them as dream fragments that serve to remind us of the need to listen and change our life. Symptoms are often the result of unfinished dreaming. Your unconscious is always dreaming the images of your life and reflecting the desires of what lives in your soul.

As the poet Rumi says, "What we fight with is so tiny. What fights with us is so big." We must find the way to end the fight and enter where our heart truly lives.

CHAPTER 8

When Your Heart Is Broken Open

*Grief and the deep, slow process to which it yields have
a rhythm of their own, and to refuse to sink into
those rhythms is to make a monument of a
past which no longer has a future.*
—ROBERT ROMANYSHYN

W ho among us can grasp the enormity of the anguish and sorrow that continues to roll out, wave upon wave, from the World Trade Center bombing? Who among us can even grasp the Mystery as it unfolds—linking strangers across the world in the paradox of shock, grief, compassion, and love? As the first hours pass and the days unfold, we begin to hear stories of the true Mystery that is the heart—the stories of selflessness, of random acts of love and caring, of strangers who, totally unaware of one another moments before, have become connected heart to heart as deeply as lovers or relatives. And we hear the stories of an even deeper *Mysterium* manifesting its presence and connecting humanity through pain and sorrow. Like the story of Ron.

At the World Trade Center that day Ron stopped to assist a badly burned woman who was in deep distress—a stranger—who like himself was suddenly a victim of the holocaust of this September morning. Earlier, Ron's sister and her young daughter had boarded a plane from New York for Los Angeles. Happily anticipating their journey, the two—mother/sister, daughter/niece—had been on one of the planes that became the firebombs that hurled Ron into this catastrophe. Sister above, brother below, one dying while the other was fighting to save lives. Neither knowing they were united in this way. And the woman Ron saved? A stranger, but because of the intensity of those hours Ron and this stranger became linked in the Mystery that is life. Ron's heart—broken open with indescribable sorrow—finds his life indelibly inked into the life story of another. The knowledge and memory of his spontaneous, unpremeditated act of courage toward this stranger somehow balances the horror of his loss. The stranger, present in the exact moment, needed Ron as much as he needed her, and through grace and maybe even fate, they found one another. Her need, his reaching out, will somehow allow him to continue to move forward through the days ahead. Already the news agencies, attempting to make sense out of the chaos, asked the question, "How are these two lives linked? And why?"

How do any of us explain the whys of those events in life that break our hearts wide open, throwing us to our knees or flat on the ground, unable to find the solace or meaning to pull us through the unendurable? We don't. We can't. We probably never will. Our intellects cannot wrap around the enormity of the inexplicable without getting so caught up in the details that we become victims rather than participants. In the great Greek tragedies there is a profound lesson that may help us now. It is said that every character, both good and evil, both tragic and romantic—the fool as well as the sage—is needed for the drama to make sense.

What is meant by *sense?* Well,

- It is our senses, not our intellect, that teach us about our relationship to the world, to Spirit, and to life. How we feel can send our intellect reeling—our rationality struck dumb if we have the courage to be bone honest with ourself. If we can't or don't, those feelings can turn sour, mean, and destructive. There is a capacity for terrorism within each of us that may never be directed outward but can ruin life nonetheless.

- To make sense is to go inward to those deep places where we harbor our unspoken feelings and bring them into the light in order to be fully present and fully connected to that whom we are.

- To make sense is to hold ourself fully accountable for our feelings of bigotry and hatred, of indifference and self-loathing, and to allow our hearts to break open to the grief that arises when we acknowledge that these feelings have distanced us from our own humanity.

- To make sense is to realize that life is far more complex, more fickle, and more capricious than we wish to imagine. If we are without the sense of something greater than humanity at work in our life, eventually the event will occur that renders us senseless.

- To make sense is to recognize that beyond identity and acquisition and power is our profound need to relate—to love and be loved—just as we are.

Heart Sense

Our grief always has two dimensions. We grieve for *the loss* (the thing or the person) and we grieve for *my loss* (as it affects an inner sense of identity). At one time we may feel a great sense of regret about losing a job or a precious object, but we know that we will pick up the threads of life and go on, while at another time, we may feel we are less a person or we are unable to face the future because the loss has diminished us intrapersonally in some way.

We feel guilt about our secret knowledge that we are frightened or in confusion about our identity because of a loss. We attempt to shake ourselves free of the grip of discomfort and self-doubt by saying things like, "What I am concerned about is nothing compared to what has just happened." This may make head sense, but it never makes heart sense. This is what your heart feels.

- Your heart "knows" that every living thing on this planet is connected, and when we grieve we are grieving not only for others but for our own loss.

- Your heart knows how often you visit its sanctuary and what you have found there. You cannot fool your heart into a pretense of not needing God or love or compassion. Your heart knows better and will intensify its aching to wake you to the reality of your unexplored spirituality.

- Your heart senses your profound need for contact, for reassurance that you are not alone, that there is meaning and purpose in your loss, and it will compel you to reach out even as you are wishing to run, to escape, to wake up and find that the sorrow has all gone away.

- And, your heart senses the embodied resources you have not yet called upon. It breaks open to make room for the depth of your sorrow *and* the ever-present energy of healing to enter your heart at this time.

- A heart broken open is not a shattered heart. It is a heart unafraid to shed tears, unafraid to be vulnerable, unafraid to weep, unafraid to name its own demons and to refuse to project them onto others.

- A heart broken open is a heart full of receptivity to the healing love of strangers, of animals, of prayer, of compassion, and of memory.

- A heart broken open offers you a sanctuary in which you can find God so that you are never alone.

- A heart broken open links you forever to the family of humanity.

- A heart broken open is an invitation to become real—to stand before the altar of your soul and pledge that you will no longer waste this precious life on unconsciousness.

In chapter 5 I wrote about the contrast between destiny and fate. I wrote about destiny as an ability to live life consciously and conscientiously, intentionally developing an inner connection to the Ineffable. And I described fate as living life never soul searching—never holding yourself accountable for your choices in life—never seeking a connection with something greater than your ego. Fate is a life lived in resignation, passively taking what comes, being a victim of life's whims.

When the unendurable happens, we are inclined to feel as if fate has taken over—that influences beyond human control or understanding are at work. Yet, after every catastrophic event, if we are able to gather the stories we soon realize that destiny, not fate, is on the move. Nature shows us that the lushness of life has to be replaced by dying, death, and decay if life is to endure. The lesson is easy to take if it is not one of *my* loved ones cut down prematurely, not *my* life that becomes deadly and decaying.

Mythology helps the human psyche understand and accept what is too complex or painful to face head-on. What the story of the Fates (the Spinner, the Weaver, and the Thread Cutter) teaches us is that even as one is cutting a thread of life, as death calls, another is spinning a new life into being, while the third is weaving *all three* cycles into the meaning of your life and the tapestry of humankind.

It is so easy to miss the relatedness—that fate and destiny are linked—that life and death serve the same good. During the aftermath of the WTC attacks, I heard the reassurance of this myth as it came alive right here, right now.

One of the national news channels tells this story. On the morning of the eleventh of September, a child has died at Vanderbilt University Hospital in Tennessee. In the midst of the family's grief they have donated this child's liver to an organ transplant program. The Weaver has already begun. The surgeon hears the news of the bombings and that all national air space is closed as he begins to prepare to remove the child's donated liver. Meanwhile, in Houston, Texas, an infant is waiting—her life is suspended by a thread—in critical condition. The donor's liver is a match, and this infant's life depends upon receiving it. The hospital authorities call and ask the Federal Aviation Authority for some direction, for help. The Spinner is holding her thread of new life fast, waiting for the Weaver to pull all these many threads together. A flight crew from the East receives permission to fly the organ to a hospital in the West. The Texas infant's thread of life is spun anew—woven into the tapestry that two hours ago was unseen, unanticipated, and could not have happened had the WTC bombing not occurred. We are all connected in so many ways—heart to heart, soul to soul, thread to thread. As one heart breaks open, another is healed. And, as a heart is healed, so another is breaking.

Naming Our Gods

The two words we heard repeated most often during the WTC disaster are *love* and *God*. More than sixty-two nations lost citizens in that event. Many nationalities, many doctrines, many ways to call upon God, to offer up prayers, and to extend love. The one common bond is the universality of heart-centered love. I have no doubt that on this particular September Tuesday thousands who may never have felt a need to turn to God, to allow their hearts to break open to the sustaining love of the Universe, did so in spite of themselves. And in so doing, as they said the words, "Oh God," they made heart sense.

There is no such thing as a Holy War. Nor is there such thing as a black heart. There are unholy wars fought in the name of God and there are intellects so blackened by hatred and ignorance that their deeds are heartless. Over and over we must come to terms with our individual role in the tragedies—how our life makes "sense." And as we seek answers to these questions we must be prepared to allow our heart to be further broken open. "Our life," reflects author Annie Dillard, "is a faint tracing on the surface of mystery. The surface of mystery is not smooth anymore than the planet is smooth."

Calling in the Dark Gods

Do you know their names, these so-called dark gods? They are the stewards of bigotry, of ignorance, of hatred, of greed, of indifference, and of entitlement. They are the misbegotten children of ideas and attitudes and intentions that have shallow roots, and so their parents rush to transplant them in virgin soil where like weeds they can wreak a tangle of brambles and fallen blossoms. None of us, no one, is immune to giving these seeds ground upon which to grow. Words will not root them out. Laws will not eradicate their presence nor their influence, because the source ground from which they spring is within each of us. Subtle, the first shoot may begin with an unexamined opinion or an agreement. But all these dark gods need is a tiny crack in the ground of your beliefs—a small opening in which to cast a seed. Seeds can lie dormant for many seasons, waiting for the most advantageous conditions before they spring to life. We cannot root out that of which we are unaware. We must begin with the obvious.

HEART NOTES

Unearthing the Dark Gods

You will want your CD player, a piece of music (see Resources at the back of the book), your mirror, two chairs facing one another, a lot of paper, ans a pen or pencils. Before you begin, make this pledge to yourself.

> I, _____ , pledge to myself that I will be uncompromisingly honest about the dark gods I have given access to in the sanctuary of my heart. As I enter this sacred and private space I will neither deny nor criticize myself for what I find growing there. Instead, as in the past, I will be transparently honest about my beliefs and feelings as I take charge of what I know and believe about my self.

- Now, make a list of anything you feel you hate. Food, persons, colors, nationalities, anything. Be honest. If you say you hate the taste of water and never drink it, put this on your list. You are about to discover how often you use this word, *hate,* and how much it influences your capacity to love freely.

- Now begin your weeding. Many times we use the phrase, "I hate," when what we mean is *I am afraid of,* or *am ignorant about, feel shamed by,* or *vulnerable to.* Go through your items one by one and decide if anything you have listed might more honestly fit in one of these categories. Maybe they fit under two or more.

- When you have distilled your list down to those things you genuinely feel you hate, you are ready to get real. Place your mirror on the chair opposite yours, and choose one item from your list. Now, either speaking aloud or writing it down, be totally honest about why you hate this particular thing. Keep writing or talking until your body tells you that you have fully expressed your true feelings. Remember, these are your feelings and you have every right to have them. Now imagine that your heart is seated in the chair across from you. Your heart loves you and fully understands you as no one or nothing else can. Move to the other chair in order to speak from your heart.

- Picking up your mirror, look deeply into your own eyes and ask your heart to free you from this hatred. Ask your heart to speak. Now tell your story from your heart's perspective. When you are finished, put your mirror on the seat of your chair and move back to the first chair.

- Ask yourself, "What of my hatred has changed?" Now tell your heart about the changes. And once again, talk to your heart about your hatred. Be certain you feel that you are listening to yourself and really hearing yourself without judgment, no matter how impassioned you feel. If you still have hatred, tell your heart why and ask your heart to hear you.

- Now move to the other chair and pick up your mirror, and allow your face to reflect your hatred. Really look into the eyes of this face. Do they match the eyes of your heart? Ask your heart to break open and teach you how to release this hatred and become something greater than this. Ask your heart to speak. Put your music on and allow your heart to move you as you dance a body prayer of transformation, releasing the energy of hatred and opening to the energies of compassion.

When you have finished, go and wash your hands and face and promise yourself that you will not let your heart's wisdom go unheard or unappreciated. David Whyte, the poet, says that "there is an energy in

this universe that heals, and it heals because that is what it does." You
can trust this energy with all your heart.

When Hope Disappears

How often have you spoken one or all of these sentences? "I won't
give up hope. If I give up hope, I feel I am letting them all down."
Or, "I have nothing left but hope. Without it I will go mad." Or, "I
cannot bear to relinquish hope."

What can you do when hope disappears? What can you cling to,
rest upon, when hope is extinguished? Hope helps us sustain the
reality of the past and the promise of the future. Hope gives us the
fortitude to weather the worst with its promise of relief. And when
we realize there is no relief—that what is, *is*, then what? Have we
no recourse but to turn to hopelessness?

Hope has many faces—many strains of relief. After we are faced
with the realization that what we have hoped and prayed for is not
to be, then we must take our broken hearts and spirits to hope's
strong sister—faith. We can have faith for faith alone—not knowing what the next hour will bring, only that there is a design, a pattern, a purpose in life that is being enacted right here, right now, in
our life. Faith doesn't require us to believe in anything—or to give
up anything. Faith offers us a thread to hold fast to while we are
loosening the grip of our nightmare, awakening to the permanency
of this grief.

Faith, like love and hope, has the radiant connecting qualities
that give us the first glimmer of meaning after a meaningless event.
No one can ever be present at a birth without believing that there
is a miraculous story being told. Faith is the energy that banks the
embers of that miracle—keeping them alive until we are ready to
relight the fires of our passion for living. Faith makes meaning from
the meaningless.

A Mantra to Faith

T. S. Eliot, the poet, reminds us that when we have lost hope and love there is still faith. The capacity to wait without hope or love, until the new energy that can bear the loss emerges, is an act of immense faith. The new life waiting to emerge from the ashes is held in the pregnant embrace of the waiting. This exercise will give you an anchor in faith until other energies emerge.

- Find a place where you can sit undisturbed and comfortably. Place your journal on your lap and write the following mantra in it:

> Even though I cannot believe in the goodness of this world, I cannot bear the pain I must bear, I will have faith in this journey knowing that when reason fails me my heart of its own accord is Spirit-centered. If I can find nothing that gives me hope I will turn to Nature and dig in the soil— aimlessly if I must—and have the faith that Nature in her ancient wisdom will offer me healing. I will not allow this pain to rob me of my one and precious life. Even when I can find no reason to continue to go on, I will place my faith in my heart's true purpose and allow my heart to break open with my sorrow. I will take my sorrow to the altar of my heart and await the renewal of life.

- Reread this commitment aloud and allow this promise to take root in your heart. Trust that your heart will listen and show you the way.

The ego expects rapid change and limited pain. Your heart is far more realistic, knowing that pain is the harbinger of change. New consciousness often brings us psychological and emotional pain until we have made the changes necessary to meet the discomfort.

Do not give up on yourself, ever. Think of the discomfort as spiritual growing pains.

The Cycle

One year. You must allow yourself one year before you can begin to step fully into your changed life. During this year you will often revisit the memories of the year leading up to the event that marks the change. Psychologically, you will probably remember by telling yourself that "last year" or "only a year ago" your life was different. After a full cycle of consciously noted anniversaries has passed, your entire system will be more receptive to releasing these events to the past and to acknowledge that you have entered a new phase of life. This is called the "anniversary effect." We tend to make meaning of certain events by either comparing them with the past or anticipating their repeat in the future. When there is a loss, the first year of remembering usually carries the most impact because it is the first "anniversary" of not having the familiar pattern available.

Consciously acknowledging the effect of a loss is a major step toward taking responsibility for how you live your life. Obvious or not, your destination is toward life and consciousness and away from denial and unconsciousness. Yet sorrow repressed is sorrow wasted. Sorrow, like all intense feelings, must be cared for gently, respected for its potency, honored for its integrity, acknowledged for its honesty. The ordinary life is filled with small sorrows, illnesses, separations, aging, and time lost or misspent. When a sorrow keeps knocking at the door of your consciousness you do not benefit by forgetting—you grow and are deepened by integrating the full experience slowly. And always sorrow transforms into hope as it is spoken about—shared—held within the circle of love. Our rituals for mourning the passage of time and relationships offer us membership in this circle. Funerals, birthdays, wakes, shiva, memorials, poetry, song, gatherings, and story are all deeply healing, releasing us from having to make our way alone. In truth, all acts of remembrance and conscious letting go reaffirm our commitment to the circle of life.

One year. Give yourself or another person one year to release what has passed fully and deeply and with integrity. One year—with no expectations. Our intellects have to revisit each day of that year, remembering that only a year ago life on this day was still irrevocably unchanged. Then the day will dawn when it is a different year—there is a different quality to the remembrance.

HEART NOTES

365 Days of Remembrance and Gratitude

You can begin your intention to create a heart-guided quality of gratitude in your life, no matter how great or small your loss, with these simple steps.

- Hang a calendar that displays the entire month on one page where you cannot miss it.

- Each day, make yourself acknowledge something for which you are grateful and write it on your calendar, even if you do not want to or cannot see any reason to. Do it. Bart wrote, "Today I shaved. Not because I wanted to but because I have nothing else I want to do either." That's a start. In the simple routine of shaving Bart remembered how his partner loved the smell of his aftershave, and he felt a smile cross his face for the first time since Aaron's death. This is a step toward life.

- At the end of each week, reread what you have written for the week and bless it.

You are not doing this for yourself alone. We forget in our grief that what affects our life is also affecting others, some of whom we may never know. As you do this for yourself you are doing it for others. And, as they engage their grief, they are also doing it for you.

Grief's Blessings

Callie writes,

When my husband and I found out after ten years that I was pregnant we were ecstatic. We felt the humility of two whose prayers had been answered. Our son was a continuing joy, and our lives were filled with the happiness of the present and plans for his future. What began as a joyful outing turned into a nightmare when my husband and son were killed in an accident. I was unable to eat or see anyone or even get out of bed. I spent my nights wishing for morning and my days praying for the night to come. I felt horribly tricked—given the world only to have it snatched away without rhyme or reason. Cards came. Letters, telephone calls, e-mails, visits, but there was no one at home in my body—no desire to connect or be touched.

One Saturday my toilet began to overflow and because it was the weekend I felt the hopelessness of getting any help at all. As I called one plumber after another, my doorbell rang. Who now?! Opening the door I saw a pizza delivery man. I hadn't ordered a pizza. In a tumble of words, I told him he had the wrong address and that my toilet was overflowing and as I spoke the tears leapt from my eyes and I sank to the ground.

This "misdirected" delivery man asked me for my toolbox, and when I pointed to the basement he asked if there was a dog. As I shook my head No, he descended the steps and emerged in minutes with what he needed. In no time at all he fixed the toilet, made tea, and insisted that I have a slice of pizza.

Mark, I'll call him, was an advertising executive who had quit his job and started delivering pizzas after his wife of thirty years died unexpectedly. He had confused my street address with one two blocks away. Two strangers, one pizza, and a clogged toilet. Before the night was over we cried and held one another in shared grief and compassion. Mark has been in my life for ten years now, and we often smile in gentle disbelief at how it took our profound losses to lead us to one another—or—from our profound grief came the miracle of our sharing.

Three Degrees of Relationship

Life is a multilayered complexity. As the world becomes a village, each life is separated from others by fewer than three degrees of relationship. We are all connected in so many necessary but inexplicable ways. When we are in shocked disbelief, it is difficult to remember this. Community and shared stories—not advice, but experience—help. Many times, if it weren't for a shared story we would never hear the rest of our own story.

Emily was diagnosed with cancer and immediate surgery was recommended. She had only a week from her diagnosis until her surgery. Her days were a mixture of practical concerns and endless prayer for her own safety and the safety of her family. After her successful surgery her surgeon told her this story. On the other side of the wall separating Emily from the room next door was a patient who had had the same surgery as Emily. Both women were in their forties, both had curly jet black hair, both had grown children. Emily lived and the other woman did not. Emily's surgeon said, "Emily, I don't know what plans you have for your life, but I want you to know that your life is to be lived. Go and do so." Emily never learned who the other woman was. "I felt," she said,

> that the details were not the point. What I heard my surgeon say is that for reasons I could never know, nor could he, that woman and I had made a transition together. I was chosen to stay and she to go on ahead. You see, that's what I believe life is all about. Finding meaning enough to sustain us in the easy and the difficult times. So every time I feel myself filled with the fear of this cancer returning I pause and fill my heart with gratitude to this

other woman—a part of myself, maybe—a stranger that joined me to teach me how to make sense from my life.

Gathering the Reassurances

Life is filled with spontaneous events—coincidences that can leave us marveling at their timing and significance. These gifts come to us unexpectedly, seemingly unbidden, and often unnoticed. This exercise is an invitation to notice them. Treat them as welcome guests come to teach us we are loved. First, intentionally create a delightful space for yourself. Do not cut corners. If you love mango iced tea and you have none, delay this exercise until you get some.

- Put on a garment you love. Find a beautiful container and fill it with something you love to drink. This party is for you and your soul; make it special. Take your mirror, your journal, and colored markers and find a comfortable spot near your CD player. Choose a CD you are fond of and put it on.

- Now review the past few weeks and begin to note the coincidences that have occurred. Choose different colors to record each event—the traffic light that stayed green when you were rushing, finding the last loaf of your bread left in the store, or the telephone call that came at the last minute. This will take some practice, but it is worth its weight in happiness when you begin to recognize that there are "angels everywhere."

- As you uncover these treasures—and they are present even if you have difficulty recognizing them at first—allow your heart to expand with your capacity to take delight in your life.

- Read each one and, looking in your mirror, take delight in the reflection you see there. These are the eyes that can see beyond loss, beyond black and white. These are the eyes that can recognize the gifts of Spirit.

- Decorate this page with all the colors that please you, and promise yourself to add to this list until you no longer need to because you are awake and aware of the presence of these gifts as they come your way.

You can view your life as black, white, and gray, or you can allow yourself to see the many colors that are awaiting your inner vision. When your heart is broken open, be gentle with yourself; you are never alone. When your heart is bruised and battered and this life offers no retreat, remember that your soul and the world's soul, your heart and the world's heart, are linked in steadfast love. There are angels everywhere.

Grief knits two hearts with closer bonds than happiness ever can, and common sufferings are far stronger links than common joys.

—ALPHONSE DE LAMARTINE

CHAPTER 9

When Your Heart Celebrates

I choose to inhabit my days, to allow my living to
open me, to make me less afraid, more accessible,
to loosen my heart until it becomes a wing,
a torch, a promise.
—DAWNA MARKOVA

Parties, parades, wakes, obituaries, births, old age, change, remembrance, each one providing the swell of life's tides—the ebb and flow of past and future collects in the here and now. We celebrate to remember, to let go, to move on, to laugh, to dance, to mourn. And always our heart is noting where and when and how we celebrate as it marks the passage of our days and gathers the vibrations of our quickening and our waning, all the while tracing the fragments of our celebrations into a map of peaks and valleys—the topography of our inner terrain.

When your heart celebrates your life, it calls upon a syntax of expression and a lexicon of resources that are quite different than the expressions and the choices made by your head. Your heart celebrates by valuing castoffs; by noticing gestures; by casting an ancestral net; by remembering the unforgettable; by relating to what *matters*.

Valuing Castoffs

An ordinary cardboard box filled with discarded clothing, hats, jewelry, and bits and pieces of fur, feathers, scarves, and shoes is waiting, just waiting for the celebration to begin. All celebration begins with the imagination. As the kindergarten children gather, the teacher says, "We are going to a party for Peter Rabbit's birthday. Can you make a birthday party for Peter?" Hands eagerly dip into the box and pull out the contents. An old gray scarf becomes Peter's lovely fur coat; two orange tennis balls are "round" carrots brought by Farmer MacGregor as a peace offering on this, Peter's Day. Fabric takes on a new lease on life as it is imaginatively woven into the celebration. A discarded tube of paper becomes a flute, and the piper begins to lead the celebrants in a winding dance down the "garden path." Two slippers create a soft tympani in accompaniment as the mystery of the imagination becomes the magic of celebration. Off to one side a box of Kleenex and a bag of buttons become individually wrapped gifts, one for each celebrant. "Here," says the gift giver, "Peter wants us each to have our favorite thing." Unwrapped, buttons become metaphoric treasures—jewels, toys, bullion of the soul. For over an hour the transformation continues until the energy reaches its natural end. Everyone has juice and cookies, and amid much laughter the bits and pieces are returned to the box for safekeeping, to await another invitation to become a cornucopia for the imagination, a celebration from the heart. Magic, metaphor, and mystery, the shimmering of possibility, of promise, lie side by side, pregnantly awaiting discovery.

Celebration is pure metaphor come alive in the body, in the moment, in the air. Our imagination urges us to step just beyond the bounds of routine and rationality and live from the depth of feeling that is stirring us into movement and expression. Metaphor, that fluid, bridging energy between our intellect and our imagination, which can turn a cardboard tube into a wondrous flute, emanates from the heart's knowing and awakens within us the capacity—the desire—to see beyond the confines of the obvious, the evident. Metaphor elicits story where it is needed using the language of image and reflection. "Celebrate the night!! Come on!" the song invites us to step into the dance and follow the heart's lead.

When our spirit flags and our energy drains away, a single metaphoric spark can simultaneously interest the mind, energize the body, and evoke the imagination. The heart's beat quickens—this is where the soul is enlivened. What only moments before was lusterless and bleak becomes multifaceted and reflective. A broken heart, the face we cannot bear to look into, or the drabbest of days is transformed and rejuvenated—revitalized. Celebrate! Dare to take your box of discards, of castoffs, and magically evoke the mystery that is your life.

The Mystery of the Imagination Evokes the Magic of Celebration

Children seldom if ever draw a tight line between reality and imagination. They allow the two to blend as needed so that on a moment's notice the impossible becomes the probable and the ordinary allows spontaneity to bubble through. A child can create a celebration on the spot and thoroughly enjoy every moment. As adults we hold back and wait until either the celebration is created for us or we have a good enough reason to yield to the imaginal. Mostly our reticence is rooted in our confusion between magic and mystery. We tend to think of magic as a trick—an illusion whose appearance, if unquestioned, will make us feel foolish in the end. We are charmed when a magician takes the same box of discards that our school-children used for Peter Rabbit's birthday and turns the contents into rabbits and jewels—yet we aren't fooled, this is no celebration of a mystery. It's a trick and so we keep our distance, charmed though we may be, so as not to get caught living in the moment, transparently naive and easily duped. In fairy tales we are warned to beware of black magic—the tool of spell casters and omen makers. And then, magically, the fairy tale uses metaphoric sleigh of hand to teach us its message as the frog becomes the prince and the pealing of the midnight bell sets the entire kingdom on a search for the bride-to-be. Magic, the close cousin of mystery, has gotten a bum rap.

Actually, our negative attitudes toward magic have done much to dissuade our culture from spontaneous heart-inspired celebrations. If we follow the trail of magic back to its origins, we find ourselves in the realm of the Greeks, the Romans, and their neighbors who valued magic, from whose energetic roots came philosophy and many of the imaginal arts. Illusion does not always have to be a trick. There is beauty and great healing potential in the ability to celebrate life by creating an expression of the mystery in a magical way. We do this with our parties and our holidays and certainly with our church rituals. There is no deeper mystery than the "magical" transformation of the bread into body or the wine into blood. When we happily invite the celebrant to blow out the candles on the birthday cake—but make a wish first—we are evoking a bit of magic, while also creating a celebration that honors the mystery of life and the seasons of living and the blessing that one has made it past another milestone on the journey. Our eyes twinkle and our hearts quicken in the pleasure of our mutual collusion.

Magic, a mysterious quality of enchantment, does cast a spell, and when it joins with the imagination we tap into a pure heart-centered celebration of life. The transformation is alchemical—life changing—at a cellular level. A mystery is something that baffles, eluding understanding, but no less alluring because of the confusion. Mysteries are magical, and magic can be very mysterious, disconcerting, confusing if held up to the standards of the head—to logic and rationality. "No, no," we would have to tell the children. "This is only a piece of cardboard tubing. It cannot make music. Don't be *absurd*." To be absurd is to welcome, believe in even, the irrational. And when the irrational is in celebration of the heart, accompanied by an invitation to trust the imagination, why wouldn't we?

In his small treasure of a book, *Ecstasy,* Robert Johnson takes us into the origins of the human need to celebrate. He reminds us that myths and dreams are both products of a fundamental urge in the human psyche to describe the relationship of the personal life to that of spirit. Both appear to be filled with imaginary creatures, magical outcomes, and irrational dialogue, yet they reflect back to us the delightful and often awe-inspiring possibilities that are available to us when we allow the mundane to alchemically transform into the *Mysterium*. This journey leads us to joy. And joy awakens in us "a long forgotten part of ourselves that makes us truly alive...." You cannot create this transformation by calling upon your head—this is an affair of the heart. While your head is trying to puzzle out how to make a cardboard tube look like a flute, your heart is already engaged in listening to the music and joining in the dance. Pure mystery, nourishing magic.

Did you know that most of us carry a dual sense of how old we are? Yes, there is our biological age, and then, internally—in our heart—we have another age. This why so often as we age we are surprised to look in the mirror and see how we look—our internal picture for that moment just isn't the same. The biological age is measured in clock time—*Chrono*logically. The heart's record is on *Kairos*'s wheel—sacred timelessness. Ask yourself, when you think of your energetic self, how old do you imagine yourself to be? Come on, participate in a bit of embodied magical exploration. If you are baffled by this question, ask yourself how old you'd rather be. This age is your interior sense of age. For me it's thirty-seven. My heart loves the idea of my thirty-seven-year-oldness. Remember now, this isn't a literal reality—it's imagined—but *real* to my heart and me.

This isn't about strength or beauty or any of the physical properties I had at age thirty-seven. Like the cardboard tube, for me, thirty-seven is full of heartfelt imaginal vitality. So, periodically I become "thirty-seven." I open my heart and invite my mind to join in the celebration. My energy shifts and I feel happy—revitalized, centered, heartful. Try it, you'll see. The experience is mysteriously magical!

HEART NOTES

Spontaneity and the Heart

It may surprise you to learn that the place where you live is much like the box of promises and possibilities that started the children on their celebration. Magic is everywhere when the ordinary is viewed through the lens of the imagination and is delighted in by your heart. Step into this exercise with a trusting heart and the imagination of a five-year-old. You'll want your journal and a table you have cleared off.

- Go from room to room in your house or apartment choosing a single object that you love from each room. Place all these objects together on a table.
- Now, using only these objects, create an entirely different way to perceive or relate to them. It can be a scene, an altar setting, a new way to arrange them—allow your sense of imagination to lead you. Be daring, be playful, be extravagant, be openhearted.
- When you are finished, check with your heart—how do you feel?
- Now, using these same items, create something to celebrate the memory of someone you know who has died. How do you feel? Write your feelings in your journal.

- Again using these same items, create something to celebrate something you love about yourself. When you are finished, reach for your journal and describe your experience.

What have you found out about your ability to allow your imagination to express a celebration from your heart? Your heart celebrates self-discovery as much as it celebrates anything you do. Do not limit yourself to a narrow range of experiences because you fear the outcome or you feel your life is much too ordinary. Look around—*your resources are everywhere, disguised as the things you take for granted.* I hope you found that when you consciously choose how and what you celebrate, you become creative in a heart-fulfilling way.

Reading Gestures

Every ritual, no matter how somber, is a celebration of something. Every celebration, no matter how spontaneous, contains a quality of ritual. This quality of ritual is why you will feel yourself drawn deeper and deeper into a celebration that speaks to your heart. When you feel the invitation your very nature responds, and passive observation on these occasions will never do. There is that instant when a certain gesture captures your sense of celebration and you know that you have to join in, body and soul. So often we flick aside the invitation. While listening to music suddenly your body can't keep still— every cell wants to join in the celebratory gestures of movement. Your feet are already engaged but your head warns you to keep your seat. Pity. The spontaneous celebrations of life are vital for your heart's sake. They are mini-moments of refreshment, reassurance, revitalization, a return to joy.

I have a favorite ritual that carries such a celebratory quality I would regret having to give it up—washing the dishes. Yes, washing the dishes. The water has to be hot and the suds rich and frothy. The light above my sink creates rainbows of color, gestures of magic, on the surface of the bubbly suds. The texture, the temperature, the focused dance of washing, rinsing, and draining each item is pure pleasure. The moment I enter my kitchen to begin a meal I fill the sink whether I plan to wash anything or not. The gesture of reaching for the faucet begins this lovely body-suds-water-soul ritual. Curiously this ritual has created more interested commentary from my family than anything else I do—and my life is varied enough and creative enough to provide them with many other opportunities. So I've learned to deflect this attention away from my affair of the heart, and in so doing I keep the joy intact. Like the kindergarten children, I've learned that if my cardboard tube makes music I need not yield to those whose cardboard tubes are devoid of the same resonances, the same melodies. The gestures of the heart point us in the direction of soul. These gestures aren't to be found out there somewhere or learned from someone else—they have to be listened for, acted upon, and appreciated for their special magic.

Listening to the way your heart leans into a pregnant pause, the way your heart softens or shifts with the expectation of what is being offered by the imagination, the way your heart urges you to create a compassionate moment, a touch, spontaneous unabashed tears, a smile—all are gestures that will allow you to grow into your full humanity. Listening with your heart can give you just the nudge, the push, the shove, the plunge that you must have if you are to fulfill your life with gestures of integrity. Sometimes the lessons are ever so bittersweet.

"Marvin," Pele writes,

> is my best friend. He has been since we met in the second grade. He likes jazz and barbecue and loud music and crowds and sweaty athletic contests where the opponents "fight" to the finish. Two months ago he was diagnosed with a terminal illness. His deterioration was rapid, and now only sixty days later he is totally bedridden and very weak. I felt so helpless. There seemed to be nothing I could do for my friend to ease his pain or our mutual

grief that he is dying. Then, early last Saturday he asked if I would find a way to bring him some barbecue and a few of his jazz recordings. Not just any old barbecue, but the special stuff conjured up by our favorite flavor genius, slow cooked and stirred over an open pit for days. "Sure," I said, eager to do anything he wanted done. When I came back that afternoon, as I passed the nurse's station the nurse, smelling the barbecue, said, "I hope that's not for our patient. His system is too fragile for grease and spices. Why don't you leave that with me until you are ready to go?" I felt conflicted—suppose I gave this to him and he had a convulsion or who knows what? But in my heart I knew that Marvin knew exactly what he needed this hot summer's afternoon, before he died. So I thanked her and said I'd take it with me.

When I entered Marvin's room the fragrance of the barbecue had already preceded me and he was smiling. "Did you get my music?" he asked. He wanted the music cranked up loud—too loud for a hospital, so I dug out his headphones and plugged them in while Marvin listened and dipped his finger into the sauce and tasted it a bit at the time. "You remember how many times we've had barbecue and listened to jazz?" he asked. I nodded and he said, "Well, my heart wants to hear about those times so tell me what you remember and I'll just close my eyes and go there."

"Hey, how can you hear me with those earphones on?" I asked.

"I can hear you because I'm listening with my heart—didn't I just say so?"

My heart is going to break if I have to do this, I thought. I can't bear remembering what will never be again. God, is this what friendship—no, loving—another person is all about? Is this day about Marvin—or me—or both? What about how I feel about God? Am I being taught that to be real sometimes you have to go to memories that are too much to bear in order to get through the pain and the fear? So I began, knowing if I was to join Marvin in our last barbecue together I too would have to dive into my heart and keep loving what our hearts have loved about those hours spent together in the familiar intimacy of a long-term friendship that we thought would go on for years and years. As story after story unfolded, the day grew late, the barbecue cold, and the music ended but we continued—me speaking and Marvin listening. When the nurse came in and said it was ten P.M. and visitors had to leave, I kissed Marvin and as I was about to go through the door he called my name. I paused, looked his way, and he nodded and touched his heart twice. A skimming gesture but it spoke depths. His lips formed the words, "Thank you." From his heart; To my heart. Soul food. Jazz, barbecue, remembrance, friendship. God.

Putting my key in the ignition, I glanced up at the tenth floor that had been as much a home for me today as any I have ever lived in. I realized that home is always exactly where the heart is. So I promised myself to visit my heart each day and ask if I had walked through life that day as a zombie—doing things but forgetting to be awake and heartful or, had I been home no matter where the day or the tasks of life had taken me. Some days I forget but mostly I remember.

I believe that a large part of the pervasive sadness that has always tugged at my soul was really my heart sorrowing over my forgetfulness. My lack of relationship to my soul. Since Marvin and I had barbecue and I promised myself to not forget I've been filled with a quiet sense of happiness and familiarity—like I'm never alone. It's like my heart is always singing softly to me.

A *gesture,* says the dictionary, is a sign of intention or attitude. Do you know the intention or attitude of your heart?

Casting a Net: Celebrating the Ancestors

Paul Pearsall writes in *The Heart's Code,* "A love map of everyone we have ever loved may be stored forever within us in a form of info-energy imprint, infinitely reverberating sounds and a set of subtle energetic patterns stored in our cells." Further, Itzhak Bentov writes in *Stalking the Wild Pendulum* that our body radiates a field of electrostatic energy that in its turn intersects with all those bodies that surround it. These intersecting electromagnetic gestures of resonance join us to one another in a mutual dance of becoming. Ever radiating, these overlapping fields of magnetic influence connect all living things around the globe. Since energy is never lost, it is fair to say that, not unlike the mDNA I spoke of in chapter 3, every living being passes on the shared vibrational imprinting of all the preceding generations. And Native Americans remind us that we have a responsibility for ecological stewardship to the seven generations that will follow us. I am now a great-grandmother with the privilege of having known personally the two generations that preceded me and the three that have followed. So I am standing in the middle of six generations and carrying that info-energy imprint in the cellular repository of my heart. If you can accept all of this, then you are certain to feel that the integrity of your heart-centered practices will be a legacy for the generations that follow you and a healing for those that have preceded you. The "love map" of your heart casts a wide net. Celebrating your ancestors knits up the dropped threads on the loom of the Eternal.

Recently a friend of mine, Carol, wrote me a note concerning her family history and how she might create a ritual—from the heart—that would serve to heal some of her ancestral past. "I began to wonder," she wrote,

> if, as I worked with the ancestors and the sadness that accompanied their life with its particular hardships of the earlier days, with

no medical attention and etc., that wouldn't help me in releasing those things from their past that have inhibited my life. I wondered if it would help me in my own letting go of the fears instilled in me in childhood because of the fears they had learned to measure the world by. My family thought it would protect me if I learned to always anticipate and expect the worst outcome. This is no longer how I see the world or how I live my life. Learning to make this change has been so healing for me and my children that I feel I want to offer the same healing to those that have gone before me.

Just because the ancestors are in another phase of their existence doesn't disconnect us. It seems that I can take their fears and place them in my heart for a cleansing. I feel this will break the chain that keeps the old energies alive. I know since I love nature I will have to go into nature to create the rituals that will best heal my ancestral past. And I will.

I have worked with people who have healed chronic symptoms, rigid ways of thinking, and even deep historical grief by creating rituals for the ancestors whose lives they felt held the key to the beginning of their own distress. I've known others who have celebrated a return to the ancestors by reclaiming their family tree, their genealogy, their past. Much of what has been uncovered is a heart connection—an inner knowing that this person's life contributed to mine—that their being on this Earth has somehow shaped who and what I am.

Recently, while I was leaving Atlanta on a trip, the curbside airline agent who checked me in remarked that we shared the same last name. I explained that the last name was not mine but my grandmother's. We discovered that his grandparents and mine were from two connecting southern states—and both from the coast as well. I mused that somewhere along the way we'd find evidence that we are distant cousins. We both enjoyed the possibility and parted feeling warmly if briefly connected. He is an African American, I am a Caucasian. At first glance it would be easy to say we have no connections, no genetic link—yet, we also are linked, if not literally, at least as a matter of heart.

Personal Truths

What do you know about your ancestors?

- In a separate journal list all you know about the last seven generations, and make a focused effort to find out what you can about them. Do this from your heart, not your head, by acknowledging that these lives were real and without them you would not be here. Really listen to what moves or excites you about what you discover. Write this down.
- Remembering that your body contains their genetic imprint, which of their strengths are you not claiming? How can you claim them?
- When you have something you want to talk over with someone, open your heart and write a letter to the ancestor of your choice and ask for guidance. This may take several days; take your time.

Our ancestry is an unplumbed depth of inner resources. You do not have to have facts about your historical antecedents; you can trust your heart and your imagination to connect you to these roots through your heart's sensing and your imaginative musings. The most important thing is to be sincere and take seriously whatever you do in a ritual. Even if your ego is skeptical, your heart and psyche are believers. To be cavalier would be like finding gold and throwing it away because it didn't shine the right way. The properties of this "gold" are faith, love, insight, and reassurance.

Remembering the Unforgettable

One never knows when and where ancestral healing will occur. Yet each and every time it does your heart celebrates.

A daughter remembers:

> Watching him plod along behind a shopping cart at Harry's Market stirred pangs of compassion for my father. He had been an erratic, brutal, and distant parent. At eighteen I left home, vowing never to need him. But now he needed me. I was the only one of his nine children who lived close enough to stop by regularly after Mom's death. Seeing him grow more fragile and less interested in life, I tried to entice him into eating, talking, getting out, and eventually moving to assisted living, where he would be surrounded by supportive people rather than home alone. He had been an outgoing person who enjoyed people, music, and life—I envisioned him starting over. But he could not. Gradually he declined. One morning only two months after we had a big eighty-second birthday party at his new apartment with many of his friends, I got a call from his nurse—he had collapsed. When I arrived at St. Anne's the ambulance was pulling away, taking him to the nearby hospital.
>
> It was my first experience with a medical emergency and, despite watching countless episodes on TV, a shock to find I was not allowed in the ER to be with my father as he was dying. Every instinct, every physical and mental urge said to be with him in this moment. But my repeated insistent requests were refused. As time hemorrhaged out of my control, my focus seemed to pulse stronger and clearer. Whether it was what I had said or how I said it I don't know, but the chaplain's eyes met mine in a moment of recognition, and she escorted me into the room where my father's body lay shirtless and lifeless on a metal gurney. The paddles I had seen so often used by actors had a stark realness as the five or six people surrounding my dad tried to coax his spirit

back into his gray, tired frame. The signal on the heart monitor was flat, and the doctors were about to cut into his chest, only slowing when I insisted DNR papers were being faxed any moment. Meanwhile I experienced the room, the other people, the medical equipment, as a quiet blur, as if embossed into the background of this most important moment. The focus of my heart and my whole self was on my father. I laid my hand on his head. It was not yet cold, but life was absent. "Dad, it's okay. You're going on now. Look for the light." Words came tumbling out without the usual mental scrutiny, gliding on a wave of pure connection. "I want you to know we love you Dad. We all love you. Don't be afraid, just go to the light. Everything is going to be okay." I know I said many other things to his lingering spirit, about Mom being there for him, about how much value he had added to the world through his music, and his many community works, but it was as if the words came directly from my heart, never passing through my head, and I don't remember them. I do remember the feeling of peace afterward, and later the gratitude that I had this moment of resolution with Dad before he was gone. Almost exactly a year later I would become a mother, for the first time trusting my parent within. Although we had never talked about his past cruelties, nor acknowledged our years of frozen relationship, I believe at a deep level my care for Dad in his last year touched his heart and made him search for a way to give me back some of the value he had stolen in my childhood. He was ready to go, and the failure of his heart was also a triumph for us. His final gift was to jumpstart mine.

When your heart celebrates you feel filled with the mystery of life.

Celebrating What Matters

As a pioneer in the relationship between body and psyche, Carl Jung often speaks the truth of the self. In writing about inner vision, he says it "will only become clear when you look into your heart. He who looks outside dreams. Who looks inside awakens."

We've come to the end of our time together, and it is important that you celebrate yourself by asking yourself, "What about this time has mattered to me and how?" Certainly the relationship between your brain and the intelligence of your heart has been awakened. Surely you have discovered what a strong and true voice emanates from within if you will listen and trust its messages.

So let us close with one last celebration of Heart Notes.

HEART NOTES

Declaring That My Life Matters

You must first and foremost believe in yourself, in your capacity to face all the ups and downs of life with creativity and spiritual strength. We all wish for a long and healthy life and we all know that eventually we each must die. The two—living and dying—are the double helix of mattering. Your life lived from the heart, open to love and trusting in the benevolence of the Universe, will protect you until it's time to die. So be fierce in your commitment to a heart-centered life. Be fierce in your pursuit of integrity—following your inner guidance and refusing to give in or give up what your heart tells you not to. And always know that you can come back to these pages and remind yourself—renew your commitment any time you wish to.

- Take your journal, your mirror, the picture of yourself as a child, and a candle to your favorite quiet spot where you will have privacy and the space to write. Light your candle.
- Go back through your journal and review what you have written. When you get to anything that really awakens your heart, pick up your mirror and look deeply into your own eyes, pledging to not forget that this matters to you, heart and soul. Then star this page.

- When you have completed reading, make a list of the heartfelt changes you have made and promise the child in the picture that you will not let her down by forgetting how your heart's wisdom is guiding you.

- Now create some ritual with this book and your journal that will let you celebrate your mattering—your coming awake and alive to your heart's wisdom about your life's purpose—your destiny. You may want to acquire something heart-shaped that will be a gentle daily reminder. Consecrate it by holding it to your heart and pledging you will not forget what matters.

If you find yourself falling in love with your life, don't resist. Take the leap, and while you are at it allow yourself to fall in love with the loveliness of others. There are thousands of ways for your heart to teach you how much it loves you—don't miss a single one.

Broken Hearts

Hearts reach
Hearts touch
Is it a parallel self greater
than muscle and bone that
joins hearts to nurture life?

Hearts quicken when someone loved comes near.
Pavlov explained the body mechanics
but not the deep knowing
the sense of safety I feel
because you hold me in your heart.
Not the courage it is capable of.

Is the language of hearts
beyond the ken of we who split atoms?
A powerful intelligence we don't yet decipher?

There is some way I go clear across the dark sky
to a stream in northern California
There is some way our hearts connect
though my sister's is in ashes under a buckeye tree.

When the heart is broken
it is also broken open

The loss that seemed unbearable in December
carried tenderly through spring
protected from the heat of August,

the chill of October
in the gentle light of April
reveals an opening where love
like an unexpected, long awaited friend at a crowed table,
squeezes in.

—MAGGIE ANDERSON, 2002

RESOURCES

ORGANIZATIONS

Institute of HeartMath
14700 West Park Avenue
Boulder Creek, California 95006
Tel 1-800-450-9111

Journey into Wholeness, Inc.
Directors, Annette and Jim Cullipher
Conferences, retreats, tapes, and home study programs combining the
    teachings of Carl Jung and Christianity
P.O. Box 169
Balsam Grove, North Carolina 28708
Tel 828-877-4809

JOURNALS

Alternative Therapies in Health and Medicine
A Peer Reviewed Journal
InnoVision Communications
169 Saxony Road, Suite 104
Encinitas, California 92024

Journal of Prenatal and Perinatal Psychology and Health
The Association for Pre- and Perinatal Psychology and Health
    (APPPAH)
340 Colony Road
Box 994
Geyserville, California 95441

MUSIC

You may already have music that you are particularly fond of.
However, I have found it is better to use a piece that holds no sentimental memories, as a favorite movie track or dance tune or the
song that you and your first love called "ours" would. The following
pieces are a small selection to get you started. Chopin Nocturnes
and the CD by Jeri Greer are especially good for opening the heart.

And So to Dream. Mike Rowland. Oreade Music.

Chopin Nocturnes. Nos. 11 & 12. Point Classics.

Gorecki Symphony No. 3. Naxos.

Miracles. Rob Whitesides-Woo. Serenity. (1-800-869-1684).

Secret Garden. Secret Garden. Phillips.

Songs of the Soul. (Order from composer Jeri Greer, Pathways,
    P.O. Box 222, Flossmoor, IL 60422.)

Spectrum Suite. Steven Halpern. Sound Rx.

BIBLIOGRAPHY

Acterberg, Jeanne. *Imagery in Healing: Shamanism and Modern Medicine.* Boston and London: Shambala, 1985.

Barasch, Marc Ian. *The Healing Path: A Soul Approach to Illness.* New York: Tarcher/Putnam, 1995.

Becker, Robert O., M.D., and Gary Seldon. *The Body Electric: Electromagnetism and the Foundation of Life.* New York: William Morrow, 1985.

Bentov, Itzhak. *Stalking the Wild Pendulum: On the Mechanics of Consciousness.* Rochester, VT: Destiny Books, 1988.

Budge, E. Wallis. *The Egyptian Book of the Dead.* New York: Dover Publications, Inc., 1967.

Chamberlain, David, Ph.D. *Babies Remember Birth.* New York: Ballantine Books, 1988.

_____. "The Expanding Boundaries of Memory." *Pre and Peri-natal Psychology Journal.* Vol. 4. 171–89.

Childre, D. L. *Freeze-Frame, Fast Action Stress Relief.* Boulder Creek, CA: Planetary Publications. Freeze-Frame is a registered trademark of the Institute of HeartMath.

Childre, D. L., and Deborah Rozman, Ph.D. Ed. "Women Lead with Their Hearts." A white paper presented at the White House Conference on Small Business. Boulder Creek, CA: Institute of HeartMath, 1995.

Childre, Doc, and Howard Martin. *The HeartMath Solution.* San Francisco: HarperCollins Pub., 1999.

Chopra, Deepak. *Return of the Rishi*. Boston: Houghton Mifflin Co., 1988.

_____. *Quantum Healing*. New York: Bantam Books, 1989.

Conari Press. *Random Acts of Kindness*. Berkeley: Conari Press, 1993.

Cousineau, Phil. "Sudden Chartes," in *The Book of Roads*. San Francisco: Sisyphus Press, 2001.

Daviss, Bennett. "A Mind of Its Own." *Ambassador: The Inflight Magazine of Trans World Airlines*. 1999.

Dossey, Larry, M.D. Healing Words: *The Power of Prayer and the Practice of Medicine*. San Francisco: HarperSanFrancisco, 1993.

_____. *Be Careful What You Pray For . . . You Just Might Get It*. San Francisco: HarperSanFrancisco, 1997.

Duff, Kat. *The Alchemy of Illness*. New York: Pantheon, 1993.

Eliot, T. S. *Four Quartets*. San Diego: Harcourt Brace Jovanovich, Publishers, 1943.

Gendlin, Eugene T., Ph.D. *Let Your Body Interpret Your Dreams*. Wilmette, IL: Chiron Publications, 1986.

Gilligan, Carol. *In a Different Voice*. Cambridge, MA: Harvard University Press, 1982.

Gleck, James. *Chaos*. New York: Penguin Books, 1987.

Godwin, Gail. *Heart: A Personal Journey Through the Myths and Meanings*. New York: William Morrow and Co., 2001.

Gray, Henry, F.R.S. *Gray's Anatomy*. Ed. T. Pickering Pick, F.R.C.S. New York: Bounty Books, 1977.

Griffith, James L., and Melissa Elliott Griffith. *The Body Speaks*. New York: Basic Books, 1995.

Ham, John T., Jr., Ph.D., and Jon Kilmo, Ph.D. "Fetal Awareness of Maternal Emotional States during Pregnancy." *Journal of Prenatal and Perinatal Psychology and Health* 15: 2 (2000), 118–45.

Harris, Judith. *Jung and Yoga.* Toronto: Inner City Press, 2000.

Harvey, Andrew. "Revelation and Revolution: The Renaissance of the Sacred Feminine." Keynote, Fourteenth Annual Common Boundary Conference. Washington, DC, 1994.

Houston, Jean. *The Possible Human.* Los Angeles: J. P. Tarcher, 1982.

Institute of HeartMath. *Research Overview: Exploring the Role of the Heart in Human Performance.* Boulder Creek, CA: HeartMath Research Center, 1997.

Johnson, Robert. *Ecstasy: Understanding the Psychology of Joy.* San Francisco: Harper and Row, Publishers, 1987.

————. *He!* King of Prussia, PA: Religious Publishing Co., 1974.

————. *Inner Work: Using Dreams and Active Imagination for Personal Growth.* San Francisco: Harper and Row, 1986.

————. *She!* King of Prussia, PA: Religious Publishing Co., 1976.

Journal of the American Medical Association (JAMA) in Intuition 17 (August 1997).

Journey into Wholeness, Inc. "Exploring Jung's Psychology for the Contemporary Christian Pilgrimage." Box 169, Balsam Grove, NC. Annette and Jim Cullipher, Dir.

Jung, C. G. *The Collected Works* (Bollingen Series XX). 20 vols. Ed. and trans. R. F. C. Hull. Princeton: Princeton University Press, 1994.

Keleman, Stanley. *Your Body Speaks Its Mind.* Berkeley: Center Press, 1975.

Kingma, Daphne Rose. *Finding True Love: The Four Essential Keys to Discovering the Love of Your Life.* Berkeley: Conari Press, 2001.

MacArthur, David, and Bruce McArthur. *The Intelligent Heart: Transform Your Life with the Laws of Love.* Virginia Beach, VA: A.R.E. Press, 1997.

Mellick, Jill. *The Art of Dreaming.* Berkeley: Conari Press, 2001.

Myss, Carolyn. *Energy Anatomy.* Boulder, CO: Sounds True Audio, 1996.

Norretranders, Tor. *The User Illusion: Cutting Consciousness Down to Size.* Trans. Jonathan Sydenham. New York: Viking, 1998.

Oliver, Mary. *New and Selected Poems.* Boston: Beacon Press, 1992, 114.

Olsen, Andrea. *BodyStories: A Guide to Experiential Anatomy.* Barrytown, NY: Stanton Hill Press, 1991.

Oriah Mountain Dreamer. *The Invitation.* San Francisco: HarperSanFrancisco, 1999.

Paddison, Sara. *The Hidden Power of the Heart: Discovering an Unlimited Source of Intelligence.* Boulder Creek, CA: Planetary Publishers, 1998.

Pearce, Joseph Chilton. *Magical Child.* New York: Bantam New Age Books, 1977.

Pearsall, Paul, Ph.D. *The Heart's Code: Tapping the Wisdom and Power of Our Heart Energy.* New York: Broadway Books, 1998.

Pearsall, Paul, Ph.D., Gary Schwartz, E. R., Ph.D., and Linda Russek, Ph.D. "Changes in Heart Transplant Recipients that

Parallel the Personalities of their Donors." *Integrative Medicine* 2: 2/3 (1999), 65–72.

Pert, Candace, Ph.D. *Molecules of Emotion*. New York: Scribner, 1997.

Reeves, Paula, Ph.D. "Spontaneous Movement as Healer" in *The International Conference on the Psychology of Health, Immunity and Disease*. Mansfield, CT: NICABM, Vol A, 1994, 479–97.

_____. *Women's Intuition: Unlocking the Wisdom of the Body*. Berkeley: Conari Press, 1999.

———. "Midwifing the Soul at the Thresholds and Borders Where Destiny and Fate Collide." Balsam Grove, NC: Journey into Wholeness Audio. Spring 1997.

Rein, G., R. M. McCraty, and M Atkinson. "Effects of Positive and Negative Emotions on Salivary IgA." *Journal for the Advancement of Medicine* 8: 2 (1995), 87–105.

Romanyshyn, Robert, Ph.D. *The Soul in Grief: Love, Death and Transformation*. Berkeley: Frog, Ltd., 1999.

Russek, Linda, and Gary Schwartz. "The Heart, Dynamic Energy and Integrated Medicine." *Advances: The Journal of Mind-Body Health* 12: 4 (Fall 1996), 36–45.

Schindler, Karon. "The Mitochondria Connection." *Emory Medicine* (Autumn 1991), 11–17.

Sheldrake, Rupert. *The Presence of the Past: Morphic Resonance and the Habits of Nature*. London: Collins, 1988.

Sylvia, Claire, with William Novak. *A Change of Heart*. Boston: Little, Brown, and Co., 1997.

Tiller, W., R. NcCraty, and M Atkinson. "Toward Cardiac Coherence: A Non-invasive Measure of Autonomic System

Order." *Alternative Therapies in Health and Medicine* 2: 1 (1996), 52–65.

Verny, T. R. *The Secret Life of the Unborn Child.* New York: Summit Books, 1981.

Walker, Barbara. *The Woman's Encyclopedia of Myths and Secrets.* San Francisco: Harper and Row, 1983.

Wallace, Douglas, M.D. "Migration Patterns and Linguistic Origins of American Indians Traced Using Mitochrondial DNA." *Genetics* (January 1995).

Weil, Andrew, M.D. *Health and Healing.* Boston: Houghton Mifflin Co., 1995.

Whitmont, Edward C., M.D. *The Alchemy of Healing: Psyche and Soma.* Berkeley: North Atlantic Books, 1993.

Whitridge, C. F. "The Power of Joy: Pre and Peri-natal Psychology as Applied by a Mountain Midwife." *Pre and Peri-Natal Psychology Journal* 2 (1988), 186–92.

Wickes, Frances. *The Inner World of Choice.* NJ: Prentice-Hall, Inc., 1976.

Wilber, Ken, ed. *The Holographic Paradigm and Other Paradoxes.* Boulder, CO: New Science Library, 1982.

Wolf, Fred Alan. *The Eagle's Quest.* New York: A Touchstone Book, Simon & Schuster, 1991.

_____. *The Body Quantum: The New Physics of Body, Mind, and Health.* New York: Macmillan Publishing Co., 1986.

Zohar, Danah, Ph.D., and Ian Marshall, M.D. *SQ: Connecting with Our Spiritual Intelligence.* New York: Bloomsbury Publishing, 2000.

If you would like to write to the author, or wish to organize
a group of fifteen to twenty women and have Paula come and
lead a weekend for you, please contact her through her
Web page: *Paulamreeves.com*.